Genius Genes

Genius Genes

How Asperger Talents
Changed the World

Michael Fitzgerald and Brendan O'Brien

P.O. Box 23173
Shawnee Mission, Kansas 66283-0173
www.asperger.net

©2007 Autism Asperger Publishing Company
P.O. Box 23173
Shawnee Mission, Kansas 66283-0173
www.asperger.net

Publisher's Cataloging-in-Publication

Fitzgerald, Michael.

> Genius genes : how Asperger talents changed the world / Michael Fitzgerald and Brendan O'Brien. -- 1st ed. -- Shawnee Mission, Kan. : Autism Asperger Pub. Co., 2007.

> p. ; cm.

> ISBN-13: 978-1-931282-44-4
> ISBN-10: 1-931282-44-7
> LCCN: 2007922525
> Includes bibliographical references and index.

> 1. Asperger's syndrome--Patients--Biography. 2. Genius and mental illness. 3. Asperger's syndrome. I. O'Brien, Brendan. II. Title.

RC553.A88 F58 2007   616.85/88320922--dc22   0703

This book is designed in Adobe Caslon.

Printed in the United States of America.

Contents

Preface

This book presents many prominent, creative individuals, including recognized geniuses, who may have had Asperger Syndrome. The central thesis is that the achievements and failures of various historical figures were the fruit of an autistic mind-style and that this could influence the way in which autism is approached today. To this end, we offer 21 case studies, arranged in chronological order of the individual's birth. The depth of treatment varies – the chapter on Archimedes is brief due to the relative dearth of available biographical information; that the chapter on H. G. Wells is longest reflects the well-documented nature of that writer's life, as well as his enigmatic and complex personality.

Asperger Syndrome is often portrayed as a negative phenomenon – a kind of affliction or curse – but if it was an integral part of the make-up and mindset of Newton, Darwin, and Einstein, arguably science's three most important personalities, it can clearly be seen in some re-spects as a gift to humanity. Who knows when or how gravity would have been theorized, the principle of evolution elucidated, or relativ-ity formulated without the untrammeled imaginations of these great, single-minded, and highly persistent men?

The connections among creativity, imagination, genius, and autism are fascinating and are far from fully understood. Given that au-tism is a condition with a major genetic component, the old "nature versus nurture" argument inevitably raises its head; various con-tributions to this debate are surveyed in the introductory chapter. Essentially, the authors' views are that genius cannot be explained by environmental factors. Although these factors may be important in creating the conditions for genius to flourish, it is largely genetic in origin, as is Asperger Syndrome. Possible links between the two can be investigated by examining biographical material.

Not all the individuals whose lives are explored in this book could be described as geniuses, but all were highly creative in one way or another. Many of the features of high-functioning autism/Asperger Syndrome enhance creativity and general effectiveness (apart from social effectiveness); for example, the ability to focus intensely on a topic for very long periods – days at a time – without interruption even for meals, and to take endless pains. Persons with Asperger Syndrome do not give up when they meet obstacles to their creativity. They are workaholics and show extraordinary capacity for perseverance. Stonewall Jackson, one of the individuals considered here, has been described as probably the boldest leader that the American Civil War produced; he had no moments of indecision and no occasion to lament the loss of opportunities (Douglas, 1940).

We are aware of the potential criticism that we have selected only material that supports our case while ignoring or glossing over data less consistent with it. Our response is that we have marshaled and systematized a large amount of information from reliable sources that has not previously been juxtaposed in this way. The methodology used in the individual chapters is to go through the established Asperger traits, one by one, and present any available evidence that the person in question showed the particular trait. Asperger Syndrome is not a clear-cut condition: Undoubtedly some of the individuals discussed in this book present relatively obvious cases, while others are less obvious. The book's treatment reflects this. Readers can draw their own conclusions according to the strength or weakness of the evidence (i.e., the book does not attempt to prove the presence of Asperger Syndrome but merely to serve as a sound, factual basis on which readers can assess its likelihood). Within this framework, we offer our own ideas and insights, based largely on the first author's long experience of diagnosing the Syndrome. We welcome further discussion of, and contrary viewpoints to, the thesis we advance.

In the case studies, we have chosen to examine a diverse set of individuals, most of whom achieved prominence in the worlds of science, mathematics, and military action. All are men because (a) autism is a far more common disorder in men than in women and (b) in Western culture and societal structure, the vast majority of famous historical figures are men (Fitzgerald, 2005; see Note 1). We hope readers will enjoy discovering these people's lives from unfamiliar angles and that the book will enhance the perception of Asperger Syndrome as a complex condition allowing of a diverse range of possibilities and potentialities, rather than an unambiguous blight on individuals and families.

Introduction

This introductory chapter gives an overview of important aspects of creativity, imagination, genius, and autism and how these may be interlinked. First, we highlight how the concept of genius has evolved through the centuries and then consider issues surrounding genius and the autistic mindset, gender, philosophy, intelligence, the psychology of inventors, mathematics and autism, and the nature-versus-nurture question.

Views of Genius

Creative acts of genius must be original and novel and bring about a change in our understanding of a subject. In Graeco-Roman antiquity, at least three major doctrines addressed this topic: the "divine fire" or "God's touch" idea; the notion that creativity was the product of "melancholy humor"; and the Muses – the nine inspirational daughters of Zeus and Mnemosyne, described in the writings of Homer.

In discussing genius, Howe (1999) stated, "The modern meaning of the word comes partly from the Latin word *genius* which stems from *gens*, meaning family, but also from the Latin *ingenium*, denoting natural disposition or innate ability" (p. 11). According to the *Oxford Companion to the Mind* (Gregory, 1987), the term comes from the Latin *genius*, the male spirit of a household existing, during his lifetime, in the head of the family and subsequently in the divine or spiritual part of each individual.

Atkinson (1993) noted, "The phenomenon of genius has provoked thinkers for many centuries, probably because it presents itself as inexplicable. In antiquity, the Romans spoke of the genius of a person or place ... By the sixteenth century this idea had been metaphorically extended to describe the innate capacity of a person ... genius is special; it is both different and rare" (p. 1).

The *New Shorter Oxford English Dictionary* (Brown, 1993) has defined genius as "inborn exalted intellectual power; instinctive and extraordinary imaginative, creative, or inventive capacity, frequently opposed to talent" (p. 1076); it has defined talent as "frequently, skill cultivated by effort, as opposed to genius" (p. 3210).

The point that genius is not effortful is important. Howe (1999) pointed out that for Immanuel Kant, "Genius was an incommunicable gift that cannot be taught or handed on, but is mysteriously imparted to certain artists by nature, and dies with the person" (p. 1) – in the present authors' opinions, this is quite close to the truth. Ezra Pound stated, "Genius ... is the capacity to see ten things where the ordinary man sees one, and where the man of talent sees two or three, *plus* the ability to register multiple perception in the material of his art" (Atkinson, 1993, p. 1).

Creativity and the Autistic Mindset

The behavior of a person with Asperger Syndrome could be seen as being on a slightly different position on the evolutionary scale than that of "neurotypical" persons (e.g., persons without Asperger Syndrome). Persons with Asperger Syndrome are, to some extent, governed by preprogrammed patterns. Therefore, they respond poorly to environmental changes, because they cannot easily adapt to changing circumstances, but this does not necessarily mean that they lack imagination. According to Storr (1988), "Man's extraordinary success as a species springs from his discontent, which compels him to employ his imagination ... discontent, therefore, may be considered adaptive because it encourages the use of the imagination, and thus spurs men on to further conquests and to ever-increasing mastery of the environment" (p. 64). A kind of discontent or alienation is inherent in autism. Storr also pointed out, "If, unlike Freud, we assume that an inner imaginative world is part of man's biological endowment, and that man's success as a species has depended upon it, we can see that we should not merely strive to replace fantasy by reason, as Freud would have us do. Instead, we should use our capacity for fantasy to build bridges between the inner world of the imagination and the external world" (Storr, 1988, p. 66). We believe that without an autistic imagination, it would have been impossible for Newton to discover the laws of gravity. Storr (1988) noted, "Einstein's special theory of relativity depended upon his being able to imagine how the universe might appear to an observer traveling at near the speed of light" and that this is an example of a fantasy that, "although originating in the imagination, nevertheless connected with the external world in ways which illumined it and made it more comprehensible" (p. 67).

This autistic imagination, to a high degree, is biologically determined. According to the *Oxford Companion to the Mind* (Gregory, 1987), Einstein emphasized the importance of creative persons having access to their dreams, which in Freudian terms would be primary process thinking; that is, a primitive, concrete way of thinking: "The implication of Einstein's remark is that, in order to innovate, the scientist, like anyone else, must break the grip on his imagination that our powers of logical-seeming story-telling impose" (p. 172).

Creative persons with Asperger Syndrome are obsessed with fundamental, bedrock discoveries. They have no interest in being merely replicative. For them, it is creative work for creative work's sake. The creative work is its own reward. They get their "psychological highs" on their breakthroughs in creative understanding. Creative work motivates them to do more creative work, to the last days of their lives (like Einstein and Ludwig Wittgenstein, who also had Asperger Syndrome; Fitzgerald, 2004). Because of their Asperger Syndrome, they are somewhat disconnected from the external world of human beings, and are therefore not so dependent on the approval of "the crowd," for whom they often have nothing but contempt. Indeed, they frequently read very little of their contemporaries' works. Wittgenstein was contemptuous of the work of Karl Popper and found the writing of most other philosophers stupid. Creators do not conform to the values of society. Srinivasa Ramanujan, who independently reinvented much of the mathematics of the past several centuries (Feldman, 1986), had minimal education and also had Asperger Syndrome (Fitzgerald, 2004).

MacKinnon (1978) pointed out that creative individuals have a high aspiration level for themselves and their creative efforts, as well as valuing independence and autonomy, being resolute and productive, getting things done, having a high degree of intellectual capacity, and genuinely valuing intellectual and cognitive matters. They tend to be rebellious, nonconforming, critical, skeptical and not easily impressed, have unconventional thought processes, are intuitive, and have a wide range of interests. They have a measure of egotism and do not judge themselves or others in terms of popularity. They often have a sense of destiny about themselves as human beings.

The biographies of persons with Asperger Syndrome and genius always refer to their child-like qualities and immature personalities. In psychiatry, immaturity of personality is portrayed extremely negatively, but then psychiatry tends to be negative in style. Psychiatrists have never been able to see the creativity in this immaturity of personality. Feldman (1986) pointed out that as early as 1930, Franziska Baumgarten observed that the child prodigy exhibits a curious mix of child and adult qualities.

Maslow (1971) stated, "The creative person, in the inspirational phase of the creative furor, loses his past and his future and lives only in the moment. He is all there, totally immersed, fascinated and absorbed in the present, in the current situation, in the here-now, with the matter-in-hand .... This ability to become lost in the present seems to be a *sine qua non* for creativeness of any kind. But also certain prerequisites of creativeness – in whatever realm – somehow have something to do with this ability to become timeless, selfless, outside of space, of society, of history" (p. 61). This would describe indeed Asperger Syndrome creativity. Indeed, the Asperger Syndrome might facilitate this disconnection from the world so that creativity of pure genius can take place. Ghiselin (1952) believed, "Invention may be precluded by a distrust of deviation. Every new and good thing is liable to seem eccentric and perhaps dangerous at first glimpse, perhaps more than what is really eccentric, really irrelevant to life" (pp. 20-21).

Persons with Asperger Syndrome have a capacity for hyper-focusing on their topic of interest, which also facilitates their creativity. On the other hand, they can show lack of attention and be quite distractive at social events. Leisure or social activities play a minimal role in their lives and genius. For many, there is very little in their lives except work. As Storr (1988) has pointed out, most of the greatest philosophers of the Western world since the Greeks have not lived "normal" family lives or formed close personal ties. This is true of Descartes, Newton, Locke, Pascal, Spinoza, Kant, Leibniz, Schopenhauer, Nietzsche, Kierkegaard, and Wittgenstein. Storr also noted that the capacity to be alone becomes linked with self-discovery and self-realization, with becoming aware of one's deepest needs, feelings, and impulses. Thus, Schubert and Mozart could concentrate on their ideas in circumstances that others would find distracting. Storr (1988) further believed, "The artist or philosopher is able to mature primarily on his own. His passage through life is defined by the changing nature and increasing maturity of his work, rather than by his relations with others" (p. 154).

The high points of many creative persons' lives occur when they make a creative breakthrough. They also tend to show hyper-sensitivity and can appear to be paranoid. They are fascinated by abstraction and logic. Abstraction may be regarded as originating from anxiety – an attempt to create order and regularity in the face of unpredictable forces of nature. Persons with Asperger Syndrome are very much into abstraction as a way of controlling the world; indeed, Hans Asperger (1944) himself emphasized this feature.

In studies by MacKinnon, cited by Perkins (1981), "Creative individuals were more reluctant to judge whatever they encountered. Instead, there was a strong tendency to try to apprehend the thing or situation objectively and penetrate its nature. Less creative people seemed more prone to evaluate quickly and turn to other matters" (p. 270). Perkins then cited Rothenberg as reporting a tendency of creative people to think in terms of opposites or contraries and unite them in inventive ways.

Howard Gardner (1980), in his study of children's drawings, noticed "patterners" and "dramatists." The patterners "analyzed the world very much in terms of the configurations they can discern, the patterns and regularities they encounter, and, in particular, the physical attributes of objects – their colors, size, shape, and the like. Such patterners enthusiastically arrange blocks on top of one another, endlessly experiment with forms on the table or in their drawings, constantly match objects with one another, build pairs and trios and the like; but they spend little time re-enacting familiar scenes in play and engage in relatively little social conversation" (Gardner, 1980, p. 90). The dramatists were more likely to become novelists and poets; the patterners were inclined toward science and philosophy. Persons with Asperger Syndrome tend to be patterners. Patterners tend to be more introverted.

Gender and Genius

Simonton (1994) pointed out, "In the annals of science, fewer than 1% of all notables are female" (p. 33). According to Simone de Beauvoir, "One is not born, but rather becomes, a woman. No biological, psychological, or economic fate determines the figure that the human female presents in society; it is civilization as a whole that produces this creature, intermediate between male and eunuch, which is described as feminine" (Simonton, 1994, p. 37). Here de

Beauvoir is dismissing biology, which is unsatisfactory; indeed her statement is largely unreasonable.

It would appear that creativity of the Einsteinian or Newtonian types does not sit well with parenting. It is possible that creativity that focuses on the impersonal is more a male than a female characteristic. The female is the more highly developed sex in human or interpersonal terms. This would suggest that the sexes complement each other, which would be of enormous value in terms of survival of the species.

Philosophy and Creativity

Certain features of philosophical work give some insight into why persons with Asperger Syndrome would be attracted to it. Indeed, much philosophy can be seen as a kind of autistic activity. It certainly was for Wittgenstein (Fitzgerald, 2004) and Spinoza (Fitzgerald, 2005), who both had Asperger Syndrome.

According to Murray (1989), "Many philosophers insist upon autonomy at all costs, are reluctant to acknowledge debts to others, and sometimes assert that they are almost incapable of reading the work of other philosophers," and that "Kant, Leibniz, Hume, and Berkeley all insisted that their contributions to philosophy depended upon having freed themselves from the influence of their predecessors and pursued their own autonomous paths irrespective of the past. So did Wittgenstein, who is another example of a philosopher who was introverted, who particularly prized solitude, who claimed that he was largely impervious to influence, who had certainly found his main source of self-esteem in his work. He is generally counted to be the most original and influential philosopher of the twentieth century" (p. 160). All of this would be typical of persons with Asperger Syndrome.

Storr (1988) also pointed out, "Philosophers, whilst professionally engaged in expounding, refuting, and disputing the ideas of their colleagues and predecessors, seldom show much interest in their personalities or biographies, and may dismiss any interest as irrelevant, impertinent, or trivial. Philosophical systems, it may be affirmed, stand or fall in their own right, from whomsoever they have originated. This is certainly the case; nevertheless … maybe the most original philosophers of the western world were people who were not only unusually intelligent, but unusual in other ways as well" (p. 155). Again, this chimes well with Asperger traits.

Intelligence and Creativity

Howard Gardner (1997) proposed the following initial list of intelligences: linguistic and logical; spatial; musical; bodily kinesthetic; and two forms of personal intelligence – one oriented toward the understanding of other persons, the other toward an understanding of oneself. This contribution has had enormous impact by making people aware of the gross limitations of standard IQ testing.

From this list one might see autistic intelligence as linguistic, logical, spatial, and musical. Indeed, Colagelo and Kerr (1992) speculated that mechanical inventiveness combined spatial and logical mathematical intelligences.

In 1921, Lewis Terman took a view – the opposite of that propounded in this book – that high-IQ children were "advanced not only cognitively but also socially and emotionally" (Gardner, 1997, p. 23). At that time the prototype of a high-IQ child was a child who would be described as having Asperger Syndrome today, with major social difficulties, social isolation, poor motor skills and myopia, and often a target of bullies. In fact, many of the children studied by Terman became successful, professional people in middle-class occupations, but "no Terman children grew up to become creative geniuses. Two future Nobel laureates, William Schockley, who invented the transistor radio, and Luis Alvarez, who won the prize in physics, were actually rejected from the study because their IQs did not test near high enough ... Terman expected that his subjects would go on to make great creative accomplishments, but he came to realize that other factors must be involved in creative achievement besides high IQ ... having the right kind of personality and drive turns out to be more important than having the right IQ score" (Gardner, 1997, p. 285). This is where autistic features would come into play.

It is also a myth that gifted children have no social and emotional difficulties. Clearly, IQ failed to predict creativity. Standard IQ testing measures verbal and performance ability but not the other intelligences described by Gardner. The characteristics of persons of genius are closer to those of Asperger Syndrome than to those of well-adjusted, high-IQ, middle-class children. Nevertheless, creativity of genius requires an IQ of 120 or more on standardized tests.

Cox (1926), in a discussion of psychometry and historiometry, investigated the intelligence of a historical character by applying to historical data the criteria of standardized measures of the mental ability of children. Terman (1917) suggested this method. According to Cox, Terman has stated that the IQ of the child Galton could not be far from 200. John Stuart Mill was given an IQ of about 190, Charles Darwin about 155, Thomas Jefferson about 145, Immanuel Kant about 135, Michelangelo about 145, Mozart about 150, Spinoza about 130, Jonathan Swift about 125, Hans Christian Andersen about 115. Clearly, all these figures are very approximate; nevertheless, reliability coefficients of the data are available and a number of raters were involved.

The *Oxford Companion to the Mind* (Gregory, 1987) noted that many people of great creativity were only average students; the same went for Fellows of the Royal Society in London. Indeed, for renowned scientists the case is the same: Science springs to life for such individuals when they discover that instead of assimilating knowledge created by others, they can create knowledge for themselves – they are hooked from that moment onwards. This very much describes persons of genius with autism. Nevertheless, it is impossible to create mathematics of high order without a very high IQ. The same goes for physics and probably also musical creativity.

Murray (1989) claimed that we attribute the extraordinary quality of, for example, Shakespeare's poetry, Mozart's music, and Leonardo's paintings to the genius of their creators because we recognize that such works are not simply the product of learning, technique, or sheer hard work, and that no amount of analysis has yet been able to explain the capacities of the rare and gifted individuals who can produce creative work of lasting quality and value.

This is precisely our view. There is something extraordinary about genius. Its origin has to be in the genes, and it has yet to be established how this is expressed cognitively. Clearly, the products of this process can be identified. In this book we are trying to provide a clue to some of the cognitive processing that is going on in the mind of a person with genius. Nevertheless, much remains unexplained.

Inventors and Autism

The word "invention" is derived from the Latin *invenire*, which means to come upon or to light upon. Murray (1997) proposed that, "This suggests that there is something of the accidental in invention" (p. 117). Indeed, chance does play a part in quite a number of inventions. Louis Pasteur said that chance favors the prepared mind.

Inventors and inventions have, of course, a very long and honorable history. The ancients made their inventors gods; the Egyptian god Osiris taught the art of farming and the use of the plough. Prometheus, according to Greek mythology, taught the use of fire.

It is interesting that many of the qualities seen as advantageous for inventors are closely related to Asperger traits. (One of the case studies in this book deals with a great inventor, Nikola Tesla.) In a study undertaken a century ago, Iles (1906) quoted patent attorneys as listing the main characteristics of inventors as follows: originality, analytical ability, imagination, perseverance, observation, suspicion, optimism, and mechanical ability. In the same study, directors of research described the characteristics as analysis, perseverance, originality, imagination, training and education, reasoning and intelligence, competence, and observation. The inventors themselves put the list as follows: perseverance, imagination, knowledge and memory, originality, analytical ability, self-confidence, keen observation, and mechanical ability. Iles emphasized the inventor's capacity for patience, perseverance, and hard work, and the ability to accept a lack of progress for months at a time and to traverse the same ground indefatigably.

There are a great number of inventors in the engineering and mathematical domains (domains particularly attractive to persons with Asperger Syndrome) who have enormous curiosity and a compulsion to understand and to make sense of the world. They do not accept current scientific or other views of the world and often reject received wisdom. (Chapter 10 on Tesla relates a striking example of this.) They are not blinded by current theories or knowledge. They have little respect for current experts in their domain and can therefore appear arrogant, self-centered, and narcissistic. Many of them have an extraordinary capacity for visual imagination. This was a characteristic of Albert Einstein, who had Asperger Syndrome. Persons with Asperger Syndrome and genius often have great memories.

Mathematics and Autism

Mathematicians tend to have much in common with persons with Asperger Syndrome – it is no coincidence that a high proportion of the personalities featured in this book worked in the mathematical arena. The relevant characteristics of mathematicians include the following:

1. Very intense/narrow interest and focus
2. Exclusion of other activities
3. May marry other mathematicians
4. Socialize with mathematicians, mathematics remaining the focus of interest
5. Repetitive adherence to mathematics
6. Interested in music; prodigies in both music and mathematics (which have some similar properties or patterns)
7. Search for order and patterns
8. Tend to be stubborn and obsessional
9. Like here-and-now work and have the symbols to work with
10. Do not need people for long periods of time when working on a problem
11. Independent-minded
12. Fascinated by basic original questions
13. Like to control their own lives
14. Like to have freedom to do their own special activities
15. Tend to like privacy
16. Have, and are skilled at manipulating, mental representations of mathematical objects

Environment Versus Innate Ability

The notion that special gifts run in families was explored by the nineteenth-century polymath Sir Francis Galton in *Hereditary Genius* (1896), which emphasized the necessity of being gifted with very high abilities. Galton was a grandson of Erasmus Darwin and a cousin of Charles Darwin. Extreme ability does run in some families – for example, the Bachs; the Darwins and their relations, including the Wedgwoods; the Huxleys; the Barlows; and a few political families, such as the Cecils (William, Lord Burghley, 1520-1598; Robert, Earl of Salisbury, c.1563-1612; and successive generations in high positions of government in England until the present day), though this might merely be due to chance. It is extremely difficult to distinguish heredity from effects of family tradition and upbringing, yet there does seem to be some evidence for genetic transmission of special abilities. In that connection, we think that Penelope Murray (1989) gives excessive weight to family tradition.

We agree with Cox (1926) that heredity sets limits to achievement. Nevertheless, it is unusual to find more than one genius in a family. This is probably because the configuration of genes required to produce a genius comes together extremely rarely. Of course, siblings share only about 50 percent of their genes.

Cox (1926) noted that, "It was known to the author of the greatest ideal republic that the ablest citizens in the state are the sons and daughters of the ablest parents. Plato was further aware that the transmission of physical and mental characteristics by heredity would not ensure the full realization of their possibilities in the individual" (p. 155). We would agree with this (i.e., that nature is insufficient on its own without some nurture).

Gardner (1997) stated "The suggestive evidence for the brain basis of giftedness, as well as the evidence for a genetic component to IQ, makes it increasingly likely that all forms of giftedness have some biological basis. It is highly improbable that any amount of deliberate practice by ordinary people could bring them up to the level reached so quickly by a child prodigy or a savant. Also with respect to the origins of giftedness, the common-sense view turns out to be less of a myth than the psychologists' view" (p. 180). Again, we are fully in agreement.

Gardner (1997) also made the point that some traits that do not run in families may still be genetically transmitted according to a principle called emergenesis, by which traits are passed on by a package of genes, but only if the entire package is transmitted. Gardner (1997) emphasized, "The question is no longer whether genetic or environment factors determine behavior, but how they interact. It is extremely unlikely that there is such a thing as a 'poetry gene' or a 'music gene,' since complex human behaviors typically have a polygenic basis" (p. 175). Lykken (1998) also dealt with the concept of emergenesis, an extreme form of epistasis, in which a unique combination of genes may lead to qualitative shifts in capacity or ability. Genetic factors are likely to contribute not only to specific abilities but also to traits such as persistence, the capacity to concentrate for extended periods, and curiosity about certain types of stimulation. These properties may in turn affect the individual's response to educational stimulation and tuition. The result is a complex interplay between inherited traits and environmental factors.

Carl Friedrich Gauss, ranked with Archimedes and Newton as one of the greatest mathematicians, had uneducated parents, his mother was illiterate, yet he taught himself to read and to do simple arithmetic by the time he was three years old. His extraordinary computing ability was evident at the age of 10. Ramanujan, another great mathematician, was reared in a one-room hut in southern India. Lykken (1998) asks why, if the genius of these men was prefigured in their genes, it never manifested elsewhere in their lineage: "The answer is, I think, that genius consists of unique configurations of attributes that cannot be transmitted in half helpings" (p. 30). These feats, taking place so early in life, certainly suggest genetic factors.

A famous American racehorse, Secretariat, sired only one other top-class racehorse – Risen Star – out of more than 400 foals. Lykken (1998) commented, "Although emergenic traits do not 'run in families,' they are more likely to reappear in a carrier family than in a random lineage. No doubt Risen Star's dam contributed key elements of the emergenic configuration" (p. 27). An important example of such an emergenic class includes those people we call geniuses.

Gagné (1988) pointed out, "The genotype imposes definite limits on the maximum attainable level of cognitive development" and that with prodigies the "ease of learning is *the* hallmark of natural abilities. It produces speed of learning which gives rise to precocious achievements. Prodigies are the tip of the iceberg, the most striking embodiment of giftedness, but below them are thousands of others who, even if less extremely gifted, show enough advance over their peers to be judged 'innately talented'" (p. 415).

Heller and Ziegler (1998) stated that conservative figures in the field of behavior genetics estimate the amount of variance explained by individual differences in personality and cognition to be about 50 percent. Lykken (1998) noted that about half of the variance in measures of creativity has been shown by the Minnesota studies to derive from genetic variation.

Plomin (1998) pointed out that genetic factors contribute significantly to cognitive abilities and that "genetics does not mean innate. *Innate* implies hard-wired, fixed action patterns of a species that are impervious to experience. Genetic influence on abilities and other complex traits does not denote the hard-wired deterministic effect of a single gene but rather probabilistic propensies of many genes in multiple-gene systems" (p. 420).

Simonton (1991) noted that the "most eminent and prolific composers – in terms of both annual rates and lifetime output – required *less* musical and compositional experience before they began to make lasting contributions to the classical repertoire. Thus, this study seems to suggest that some musical talent can lead quickly to world-class levels of compositional expertise" (p. 424). This is probably because of their innate talent.

Howe (1999) made an assertion that is much put forward by those who propound the environmental view of genius, that is, "Geniuses began their lives made from much the same basic materials as all the rest of us" (p. viii). We attempt to show that this view is unreasonable. The major reason they are geniuses is that they began with *different* basic materials than the rest of us (i.e., the configuration of their genes is different).

Psychologists put enormous emphasis on the idea of 10 years of training and 10,000 hours of practice. The vast majority of children in the world, if they were given four times this input, would not turn into a Mozart or produce works of similar stature to Mozart's. Mozart's stimulatory musical family environment did not produce his genius but only introduced him to music. His sister was in the same stimulated family home but produced nothing like Wolfgang. The combination of genes in his make-up was clearly the important factor.

Howe (1999) claimed that sophisticated inborn capabilities simply cannot exist. In this book we set out to show precisely the opposite – that inborn capabilities, indeed, are the key to understanding a genius such as Einstein or Mozart. Howe (1999) also pointed out that "a number of psychologists have suggested that the differences between creative problem-solving and ordinary thinking are ones of degree rather than kind" (p. 188). This may be so for the lower levels of problem solving but not for men of genius such as Newton.

John Stuart Mill was a genius. "Mill … was very conscious of the fact that the intellectual qualities he possessed had to a large extent been deliberately instilled in him by his father. 'Manufactured' was his own choice of word for this state of affairs … there is no other genius for whom the term 'manufactured' is quite as fitting as it is for Mill" (Howe, 1999, pp. 119-20). We do not agree that this is so because his father was also a prodigy.

Deglar (1991) believed, "American cultural anthropology, led by Franz Bowis, declared war on the idea that differences in culture derived from differences in innate capacity" (p. 20). Alfred Kroeber, in turn, asserted that heredity cannot be allowed to have acted any part in history (Deglar, 1991). Margaret Mead (1949) explicitly maintained the radical environmentalist philosophy when she stated that learned behaviors had replaced the biologically given ones. Thus, she believed that cultural stereotypes, rather than innate genetic factors, play an important role. These statements must be tempered by the fact that we now know that Mead's Samoan research was superficial and that her conclusions were based largely on innocent deceptions practiced upon her by her young female Samoan informants.

Behaviorists also tended to be radical environmentalists. For example, J. B. Watson (1924), the founder of the behaviorism movement, said, "Give me a dozen healthy infants, well formed, and my own specified world to bring them up in and I will guarantee to take any one at random and train him to become any type of specialist I might select – doctor, lawyer, artist, merchant chief, and yes even beggar man and thief, regardless of his talents, penchants, tendencies, abilities, vocations, and the race of his ancestors" (p. 21). This is simply biased, narrow environmentalism.

Even more anti-individualistic is the Confucian view that all can be skilled and that differences in skill reflect only effort and moral commitment, not any special talents. We reject this notion. St. Francis Xavier (1506-1552) declared, "Give me the children until they are seven and anyone may have them afterwards." The thrust of this was also incorrect (even though early care and education are important), because genetic factors play a greater role as the child gets older. High-ability parents may pass on high abilities genetically and create enriched environments simply because they themselves have high ability. As Scar and McCartney (1983) have pointed out, the environment is not necessarily what acts on the child; rather, the child's genetic traits may lead the child to select certain kinds of environments.

Conclusion

Having established a general context, we will now examine the lives of 21 creative historical individuals, including some geniuses, in terms of how genetic factors (specifically, Asperger Syndrome or Asperger disorder) may have engendered and mediated their creativity.

CHAPTER 1

Archimedes
(c. 287–212 BCE)

A rchimedes, the great Greek mathematician and inventor, elucidated plane and solid geometry, arithmetic, and mechanics. He was a solitary, eccentric figure and appears to have possessed some traits that suggest he may have exhibited autism/Asperger Syndrome.

Life History

Archimedes was born in Syracuse, Sicily. His father was the astronomer Pheidias, and he is said to have been related to Hiero II, tyrant of Syracuse. "He was one of the greatest mechanical geniuses of all time, if not the greatest when we consider how little he had to go on" (Bell, 1986, p. 29).

He spent most of his life in Syracuse. According to Strathern (1998), "Archimedes appeared to have lived a normal eccentric life of a mathematician. Quiet, solitary, and quietly potty – with only the occasional spectacular incursion into the public arena" (p. 72).

After Syracuse was captured during the Second Punic War (despite the deployment of Archimedes's mechanical expertise in its defense), he was killed by a Roman soldier. There are two stories of the exact circumstances of his death: (a) that he was working on a circle in the sand and said to the soldier, "Don't disturb my circle"; and (b) that he refused to go to see the Roman consul Marcellus until he had worked out a mathematical problem, whereupon the soldier became angry and killed him.

Work

In mechanics, Archimedes defined the principle of the lever and is credited with inventing the compound pulley. He also invented an ingenious screw that was used as a water pump. The Archimedes screw remains in use in the Nile Delta to this day, and the same principle is used for raising grain and sand when loading bulk carriers.

Plutarch stated that Archimedes "Did not deign to leave behind him any written work on such subjects (practical engineering abilities and inventions) ... he regarded as sordid and ignoble the construction of instruments, and in general every art directed to use and profit, and he only strove for those things which, in their beauty and excellence, remained beyond all contact with the common needs of life" (Strathern, 1998, p. 25). Calculus, which developed out of his method, has been described as the most useful mathematical tool ever invented for describing the workings of the real world (Bell, 1998).

Some are of the opinion that Archimedes did in fact use integral calculus in his treatise *On Conoids and Spheroids*, which expands geometry beyond the rigidity imposed upon it by Plato and his mystical attitude toward forms. (Plato believed that forms or ideas were the ultimate reality out of which the world was made – a development from Pythagoras' belief that "all is number." Plato believed in God and geometry.)

Possible Indicators of Asperger Syndrome

Social Behavior

Like many mathematicians, Archimedes tended to relate to other mathematicians (e.g., Conon of Samos). A famous legend tells that he jumped out of the bath and ran without clothes through the streets shouting "Eureka! Eureka!" ("I have found it!"). This relates to Archimedes's principle that a floating body will displace its own weight in fluid. According to Strathern (1998), "Archimedes was a lonely sort of eagle" (p. 29).

Narrow Interests and Obsessiveness

Archimedes was fascinated by pure mathematics. He put in long and arduous hours of theoretical work, which established him as the finest mathematical mind for almost two thousand years to come.

Any individual who spends most of his waking life in obsessive mental activity attracts wild anecdotes, and Archimedes was no exception. According to Plutarch, "He was so bewitched by thought that he always forgot to eat and ignored his appearance. When things became too bad his friends would forcibly insist that he had a bath, and make sure that afterwards he anointed himself with sweet smelling oils, yet even then he would remain lost to the world, drawing geometric figures" (Strathern, 1998, p. 27). Plutarch stated that Hieron II, the king of Syracuse and a friend and relation of Archimedes, was not happy with this kind of behavior and "emphatically requested and persuaded (Archimedes) to occupy himself in some tangible manner with the demands of reality" (Strathern, 1998, p. 29).

According to Bell (1986), Archimedes is a perfect specimen of the popular conception of what a great mathematician should be. Like Newton, he left his meals untouched when he was deep in his mathematics.

Idiosyncrasies

In addition to narrow interests and pervasive obsessiveness, Archimedes demonstrated a number of idiosyncrasies. According to Bell (1986),

> In one of his eccentricities Archimedes resembled another great mathematician, (Karl) Weierstrass (1815-1897). According to a sister of Weierstrass, he could not be trusted with a pencil when he was a young school teacher if there was a square foot of clear wallpaper or a clean cuff anywhere in sight. Archimedes beats this record. A sanded floor or dusted hard smooth earth was a common sort of "blackboard" in his day … Sitting before the fire he would rake out the ashes and draw in them. After stepping from the bath he would anoint himself with olive oil … and then, instead of putting on his clothes, proceed to lose himself in the diagrams, which he traced with a fingernail on his own oily skin. (p. 30)

Conclusion

Although the relevant information on Archimedes's life is somewhat scanty, it would appear that the great mathematician may have met the criteria for Asperger Syndrome.

CHAPTER 2

Isaac Newton
(1642–1727)

In one list of the most influential people in history, the English physicist and mathematician Sir Isaac Newton ranks second, after Muhammad, and just ahead of Jesus Christ (Hart, 1993). Newton's ranking is not surprising because he was considered a near-deity in the seventeenth century. Many of Newton's contemporaries regarded him as a god, and few today would disagree that he was one of the greatest scientists that ever lived (Bragg, 1998).

As the founding father of modern science, Newton challenged Aristotelianism, for centuries the received wisdom on the nature of the universe (it ascribed an inner purpose to everything in nature), and was the first to explain the universe in terms we understand and use today. Working alone, he studied the nature of light and the construction of telescopes, formulated laws of motion, and invented calculus contemporaneously with Leibniz. (He accused Leibniz of plagiarism and engaged in a long and bitter dispute over priority.) He became a fellow of Trinity College, Cambridge, in 1667, and Lucasian Professor of Mathematics in 1669. In 1687, he expounded his theory of universal gravitation in *Philosophiae Naturalis Principia Mathematica*. He was appointed master of the London Mint and became a wealthy man; he sat in Parliament, wrote widely on the Bible and other subjects, and was president of the Royal Society from 1703 to the end of his life.

There is little doubt that Newton showed high-functioning autism/ Asperger Syndrome. He certainly displayed the traits of autistic psy-chopathology, described by Hans Asperger in 1944, with his odd, naïve, inappropriate emotional detachment, egocentricity, and hypersensitiv-ity, in addition to his circumscribed interests. Biographies of the genius give many accounts of his strange behavior, although earlier biographers tended to perpetuate myths about his iconic status (see Note 2). A modern biography by Michael White, *Isaac Newton: The Last Sorcerer*, debunks many of the myths and shows how Newton conspired in his own mythologizing, ever careful of his self-image and legacy. He had good reason to do so. Despite being the founder of modern mechanical theory grounded in logic, he was also an alchemist and an advocate of Arianism (see Note 3) – facts he was at pains to conceal in the climate of religious intolerance that swept England during the seventeenth century – and was fascinated by numerology and chronology.

Family and Early Life

Newton was born on Christmas day, 1642, in Woolsthorpe, Lincolnshire; he was educated locally and at Trinity College, Cambridge. His father was illiterate and died before Newton's birth but managed to leave his family well provided for. Legend has it that Newton was tiny at birth and required the greatest of care to survive his first few days of life. When he was 3 years old, his mother remarried and went to live with her new husband, an aging local rector, leaving Isaac in the care of his grandparents and making frequent but short visits to see him. The trauma of maternal separation had a profound effect on him, according to White. Newton despised his stepfather, and his resentment of his mother scarcely abated when she returned 11 years later with three children in tow, following the death of her second husband. Little is known about her relationship with her son except that she made him sole heir to the estate and wrote him a letter while he was at Cambridge expressing her maternal love.

Like many geniuses throughout history, Newton performed poorly at school, played truant, and was close to the bottom of his class. Only after he was sent away to the King's School in nearby Grantham and lodged with a local apothecary with an extensive library did an interest in learning awake in him. As the mathematician Ramanujan (who is believed to have had Asperger Syndrome) was captivated as a boy by books on mathematics (Fitzgerald, 2004), so Newton was captivated when 13 years old by *The Mysteries of Nature and Art* by John Bate. The book was to have a lasting influence on him. It showed how to make machines and devices, with an emphasis on elements of experimentation and practical skills.

Newton was clearly a natural autodidact, like Wittgenstein and other geniuses. When he first arrived at Trinity College, he had a limited knowledge of mathematics – simple arithmetic, algebra, and a little trigonometry – but taught himself advanced mathematics in a few years. Many of the great minds, such as Darwin, Einstein, Ramanujan, and Wittgenstein, had only a rudimentary technical knowledge of their subjects when first entering universities. Those with Asperger Syndrome have a liking for facts, rules, and logic, and Newton was no exception. Like Wittgenstein, he had a profound interest in logic, which inevitably extended to calculation and mechanisms.

Possible Indicators of Asperger Syndrome

Social Behavior

Throughout his life, Newton showed severe impairment in reciprocal social interaction. White (1997) described him as "a secretive man, a man coiled in upon himself, detached from the world" (p. 2). As a child he was sober and quiet, and wasted little time playing with other boys. He has been described as a difficult man and a misanthropist.

Newton showed a clear lack of desire to interact with peers. For long periods of his life, he was absorbed in his work at Cambridge and secluded from everyday affairs. He was a recluse and a loner – at Cambridge he was an extreme loner. There is no record of any personal interaction with other students, except that he may have loathed his roommate.

John Gribbin, quoted in *On Giants' Shoulders* (Bragg, 1998), sums up his estimation of Newton as a weird man who made few friends. During his time at the university Newton did little to encourage others to like him: His decision to become a money lender could not have endeared him to people, although he was not excessively interested in money, despite achieving fame and fortune as a result of his scientific discoveries; avarice was out of keeping with his religious feelings. Even as an alchemist, he was not driven by the prospect of material reward. In reality he was a small-time money lender and in later life, when living in comparative comfort, gave generously to the many relatives seeking financial help. At Trinity College he lived a life of austerity, in much the same way that Ludwig Wittgenstein did. White (1997) noted that Newton existed in a permanent state of self-imposed isolation. Living in austerity and isolation in order to pursue their interests is a recurring feature of those with autism and genius.

On first arriving at Cambridge, Newton was treated as a social inferior and made to empty bedpans and clean the rooms of the more privileged students to earn his keep (White, 1997). His mother did little to ease his financial burden, in the hope that her son would abandon his university education. His humiliation, according to White, served only to strengthen his lifelong desire for improved social status and influence.

The inability, and lack of desire, to interact with peers was most acute in Newton's treatment of students. Like many people of genius, he was a poor teacher. According to White (1997), he never enjoyed teaching and cared little for his students: "Like many men of his stature, he found it difficult to bring his intellect into line with young students or those of far lesser ability, even for a short period" (p. 164). Indeed, Newton's unpopularity as a lecturer is legendary. After he was appointed Lucasian Professor of Mathematics, "not a single student showed up for Newton's second lecture, and throughout almost every lecture for the next seventeen years (when he gave up all pretence of teaching and turned his position into a sinecure) Newton talked to an empty room, listening merely to his own voice bouncing back at him" (White, 1997, p. 164).

Newton showed a lack of appreciation of social cues. There are numerous anecdotes about how he often forgot the company he was with. When he had guests he might go into another room for a bottle of wine, forget why he had gone there, sit down and proceed to work for hours, forgetting all about the guests (Bragg, 1998). This is very like Wittgenstein, who would keep his companions waiting for hours, having forgotten about them while absorbed in his work.

Throughout his life, Newton shared close relationships – many of which were not sustained – with only a handful of people. As is often the way with people with Asperger Syndrome, he formed a relationship with a man of similar temperament, John Wickins at Cambridge (White, 1997). Wickins worked as his laboratory assistant for many years and they shared rooms for 20 years, but little is known about their time together. Afterwards Wickins became a clergyman and had little contact with Newton. White (1997) speculates that given that nature of their "clinical break," it is possible that they had a sexual relationship, although there is no hard evidence to this effect (p. 235).

Similarly, Newton formed an intimate relationship with Nicholas Fatio de Duillier, a young Swiss mathematician who came to England with Cartesian ideas but was "soon drawn into Newton's mechanical universe" (White, 1997, pp. 238-239). Their relationship lasted four years. White speculated that Fatio charmed the older man with a "blend of intelligence, flattery and imagination which interacted with a nascent and largely suppressed sexual interest on Newton's part" (p. 245). It is highly likely that Newton was a repressed homosexual, and by some twist of fate Fatio managed to bring this out. There is no evidence of any physical contact, but Newton's emotional defenses had been breached, making him extremely vulnerable. According to White, the intense relationship ended in June 1693 and was never resumed.

White (1997) also suggested that Newton may have had a romantic liaison with a woman named Lady Norris and possibly proposed to her. However, given Newton's highly secretive nature, it is difficult to substantiate the claim. The only evidence comes from John Conduitt, who supposedly copied a letter of proposal from an original by Newton.

In later life Newton did show some capacity to form fulfilling and lasting relationships, especially with John Locke, the British empirical philosopher. Newton and Locke had an immediate affinity for each other, whereby Locke became his intellectual companion. In part it sprang from a meeting of minds: Locke's philosophy claimed that all human knowledge was derived from experience. Not surprisingly, his relationship with Newton was quite intense at an intellectual level; together they were later seen as the "twin pillars upon which the Age of Reason was built" (White, 1997, p. 235). Newton opened up to the older Locke, going so far as to reveal his alchemical practices to him.

Newton networked very cleverly, through the impressive power of his intellect rather than with natural charm. Throughout his life there were men who acted as father-figures and career-enhancers for him, such as the mathematician Isaac Barrow, the philosopher Henry More, and the Cambridge fellow Humphrey Babington (White, 1997).

Narrow Interests/Obsessiveness

As a young boy, Newton was absent-minded and had a capacity to become absorbed in his interests, such as reading. White (1997) noted that he had a tendency to read a book under a tree rather than watch for straying sheep as he ought to have done. On one occasion he returned from the local town with only a halter in his hand, oblivious to the horse that had slipped it.

Newton showed extraordinary intensity of focus in his work. For him, truth did not come from social relationships but from silent and unbroken meditation, as noted by John Maynard Keynes (1947). Newton was the type of person who elevated the principles of hard work and dedication to learning as the highest hopes of humanity. He could concentrate on a single problem for many decades, and revealed, "I keep the subject constantly before me, till the first dawnings open slowly, by little and little, into the full and clear light" (White, 1997, p. 85). In contrast to Wittgenstein, who read little and paraded his ignorance of other philosophers' work, Newton studied his subject both intensively and extensively. The reason was that he was searching for the "frame of nature" or a unified theory of matter. In this respect he left no stone unturned in the pursuit of truth, even believing that alchemy, too, offered a way.

Because of his all-absorbing interest in science, he had no time for literature, art, or music; he was similar to Wittgenstein in deploring time being wasted when it could be spent on work. His assistant, Humphrey Newton (no relation), reported, "I never saw him take any recreation or pastime … thinking all hours lost that were not spent in his studies, to which he kept so close that he seldom left his chamber" (White, 1997, p. 214). When in the pursuit of knowledge, Newton neglected to eat, as described by Humphrey:

> So intent, so serious [was he] … that he ate very
> sparingly, nay, sometimes he forgot to eat at all, so
> that going into his chamber, I have found his mess
> untouched. When I have reminded him, he would
> reply: Have I! Then making to the table, would eat a
> bit or two standing, for I cannot say, I ever saw him
> sit at table by himself. (White, 1997, p. 214)

Similarly, he would continue to work "without any concern for or seeming want of his night's sleep." Humphrey recounted his sleeping habits:

> He very rarely went to bed, till 2 or 3 of the clock, sometimes
> not till 5 or 6, lying about 4 or 5 hours, especially at spring &
> fall of the leaf, at which times he used to imply about 6 weeks
> in his laboratory, the fire scarcely going out either night or day,
> he sitting up one night, as I did another until he had finished
> his chemical experiments, in the performance of which he was
> the most accurate, strict, exact. What his aim might be, I was
> not able to penetrate into … (White, 1997, p. 213)

Like Wittgenstein, Newton pushed himself to the utmost limits. In completing the *Principia,* he worked himself to the point of obsession and to the brink of self-destruction. From an early age, he had a reckless disregard for his own safety. For example, when conducting experiments on color, he almost suffered permanent blindness after looking at the sun for long periods. Blindness could equally have resulted when he performed risky experiments on light and vision: For example, he once wrote that he had put a small dagger "between my eye and the bone as near to the backside of my eye as I could: & pressing my eye with the end of it (so as to make the curvature in my eye) there appeared several white, dark and colored circles" (White, 1997, p. 61).

Routines/Control

Newton was a meticulous record-keeper in every aspect of his life: diary entries, financial accounts, and copious notebooks on experiments. White (1997) noted that Newton was obsessive from an early age; while an apothecary's apprentice, he kept "meticulous records of his experiments and noted any recipes he came across in the apothecary's books" (p. 132). Like Wittgenstein, he made numerous drafts of his work: There are often 20 or 30 drafts of a single document among his papers.

The necessity of mathematical rules and logic underpinning his empirical science was crucial for Newton. However, he applied such rules not only in science but also in alchemy and biblical prophecy. He established 15 rules to analyze the text of the Bible, whereby one key approach was to reduce everything to its simplest form.

Like many with Asperger Syndrome, Newton had no interest in sports or pastimes and wanted to control peers by having them focus on his intellectual interests. In doing so he displayed how neurotic, obsessional, introverted, hypersensitive, competitive, egotistical, arrogant, and dislikable he could be. Indeed, he demanded total control over his peers, believing himself to be the foremost scientist of the period, and was ruthless with anyone who crossed his path.

He was also quite paranoid and secretive. He became embroiled in intense rivalry with his peers and had tremendous ill-feeling toward the scientific community, especially in his early dealings with the Royal Society. This was not dissimilar to Wittgenstein's total disregard for Cambridge philosophers in the early twentieth century. Newton engaged in ruthless competitive conflicts with the astronomer John Flamsteed, the philosopher Gottfried Leibniz, and the scientist Robert Hooke. With Leibniz, as we have seen, the issue centered on who invented calculus first. Newton, in paranoid fashion, believed that it was he and not Leibniz, as Leibniz claimed. In reality, they developed it independently, oblivious to each other's work at the time.

He was also hypersensitive to criticism and could not stand being challenged over his ideas. Like Wittgenstein, he was slow to publish his work until he thought it well developed, suspicious that others would plagiarize and misinterpret it for their own advantage. After he realized the basic concept of gravity, 20 years passed before the publication of *Principia Mathematica* in 1687.

In 1672, when elected a member of the Royal Society, Newton first came into contact with the scientific elite of England. He and Hooke clashed professionally and personally and remained bitter enemies until Hooke's death in 1703. Newton abruptly resigned from the Society when he deemed that its method of verifying ideas through observation ran counter to his own, and resumed his monastic lifestyle at Cambridge. Years later, when he took up presidency of the Society, he exerted absolute control and was extremely manipulative in making or breaking the careers of his contemporaries.

White (1997) claimed that the control he exerted over organizations that he was involved with made them an extension of his own personality. Following relentless arguments with Flamsteed, then Royal Astronomer, Newton removed Flamsteed's name from various parts of the *Principia*, thus diminishing his significant contribution to the work. In this respect, Newton displayed an autistic aggression in his dealing with peers: "(Newton's aim was) *to make me come under him* … force me to comply with his humors, and flatter him … (and) *have all things in his own power*, to spoil or sink them; that he might force me to second his designs and applaud him" (White, 1997, p. 323; emphasis in Flamsteed's original).

As Newton grew older, his power and influence grew. In his eyes, knowledge was power, and, "Having now garnered the power and influence he had sought throughout his life, his ascension to the status of icon appeared unstoppable" (White, 1997, p. 293). It is not surprising that he exercised complete domination of the Royal Society. His extraordinary combativeness and misanthropy, however, were not reserved for his academic peers. When working at the Royal Mint, he soon came into conflict with the governor of the Tower, Lord Lucas. He wielded considerable power at the Mint in his dealings with "clippers" and counterfeiters. The practice of counterfeiting and coin clipping (shaving off a small portion of precious metal for profit) was widespread at the time, and Newton was extremely energetic and merciless in putting counterfeiters to the gallows. He was a harsh taskmaster and drove the workers, although he drove himself equally hard. At this time, he worked about 16 hours a day, with the same focused energy he showed in his experimental work.

Newton was a supreme egotist, obsessed with his self-image and notions of immortality. According to White (1997), he made sure that the "image he cultivated would seep into recollections and memoirs long after he had been replaced" at the Royal Society (p. 308). Having reached the pinnacle of his academic career as Lucasian Professor of Mathematics at Cambridge, Newton sought other ways to accrue power and influence, which culminated in a knighthood in 1705. He acquired a taste for official responsibility after he opposed James II's attempts to foist Catholicism on the thoroughly Protestant Cambridge. Consequently, he twice became a member of Parliament representing Cambridge at Westminster, as well as master of the Royal Mint. He also became president of the Royal Society, and revitalized the then flagging institution.

Language and Humor

In Newton's case, there is a lack of clear evidence of speech and language problems and delayed development. Typically for someone with Asperger Syndrome, he had difficulties with humor and was not given to mirth. His assistant Humphrey Newton claimed that he saw Newton laugh only once.

Nonverbal Behavior

There is no clear evidence that Newton displayed any limited use of gestures or clumsy/gauche body language or that he had inappropriate facial expressions, although White (1997) has noted his brooding, dark, piercing eyes and "stern gaze" (p. 294). Certainly, from portraits he appears to have had a peculiar, stiff gaze. It seems probable that he showed limited facial expression, considering that his assistant saw him laugh only once. Nonetheless, Newton evidently had an extraordinary effect on people. Despite his natural misanthropy, he had the power to impress, as those with genius often do.

Lack of Empathy

Newton showed a clear lack of empathy, coupled with vindictiveness and insensitivity toward his peers, in part due to intense rivalry. "For him, time did not heal: his bitterness and resentment merely festered. He had almost no capacity for forgiveness" (White, 1997, p. 340). His extreme rivalry with the scientist Robert Hooke permitted only a begrudging acknowledgment of the latter's collaboration on the experiments on light. Newton's celebrated words, "if I have seen further it is by standing on ye shoulders of giants" were double-edged, according to White. The statement is often read as a compliment to scientists who had gone before him, but in fact was a jab at Hooke – a prolific scientist himself – who was so "stooped and physically deformed that he had the appearance of a dwarf" (White, p. 187). White noted that the comment showed the "truly spiteful, uncompromising and razor-sharp viciousness" of Newton's character.

Autistic Superego

Newton possibly had an "autistic superego," as evident from accounts of his early life. Like Wittgenstein, he was preoccupied with sin and wrote out confessions of "felonies against the lord." One of these lists consisted of 45 transgressions, including "threatening my father and mother Smith to burn them and the house over them" and "wishing death and hoping it to some." Other misdemeanors included "refusing to go to the close at my mother's command," "striking many," "peevishness with my mother," "punching my sister," and "falling out with the servants" (White, 1997, pp. 17, 25).

Visual-Spatial Ability

Newton showed the excellent visuo-spatial ability commonly found in those with autism. Like Wittgenstein, he could draw well. Stukeley gave an account of his early drawings: "Sir Isaac furnished his whole room with pictures of his own making, which probably he copied from prints, as well as from life" (White, 1997, p. 21).

Newton's visual-spatial ability was particularly evident in his passion for model building as a boy – a suitably insular pastime for someone who apparently had no friends at school. He was a good practical experimenter, starting in his childhood when he made quite sophisticated toys. A working "windmill" driven by mice running round a treadmill amazed his contemporaries for years afterward. He is best remembered for building kites. According to Brewster (1855), Newton apparently flew them with lanterns attached. Later he single-handedly built a telescope, which was central to his calculation of gravity. Undoubtedly, he was a prime example of a mechanical man. Interestingly, as a boy Wittgenstein built a sewing machine and had a highly developed visual-spatial ability, too. Both were interested in light and color: Newton had a lifelong fascination with the color crimson. Indeed Newton's first experiments were probably investigations of the nature of light (White, 1997).

Religious Disposition

The religious disposition commonly found in great minds, such as those of Wittgenstein and Einstein, was evident in Newton too – he had a profound interest in religion and spent a lifetime studying biblical prophecy. Gribbin claimed that he became an unorthodox kind of Christian who studied the bible obsessively (cited in Bragg, 1998). Although Newton saw the Creator's presence in everything, he was more interested in the spiritual dimension of religion than in its received wisdoms, and this applied equally to his obsession with alchemy:

> The spiritual element of the experiment was in fact
> the key to the true alchemist's philosophy … for many
> alchemists, it was the practical process that was in fact
> the allegory and their search was really for the elixir
> or the philosophers' stone within *them* … following
> a path to enlightenment – allowing themselves to
> be transmuted into "gold." This is why the alchemist

placed such importance on "purity of spirit" and spent
long years in preparation for the task of transmutation
before so much as touching a crucible. (White, 1997,
p. 127; emphasis in original; see Note 4)

Not surprisingly given the climate of the time, Brewster (1855) described Newton's writings on alchemy as the obvious production of
a fool and a knave. Newton's work as an alchemist was anathema to
the traditional world of science and to society in general. More seriously, attempting to transmute base metals into gold was a capital
offence. According to White (1997), the story that Newton's inspiration for the theory of gravity was a falling apple was a fabrication
and almost certainly told in order to suppress the fact that much of
the inspiration came from his subsequent alchemical work.

Newton wrote a "long and clumsy book" entitled *The Chronology of
Ancient Kingdoms Amended*, published posthumously in 1728 by Conduitt (White, 1997, p. 155). In it his fascination with "numerology,
time-scales and even biblical prophecy" is evident. His chronology put
the death of Christ at 34 CE; the end of Church of Rome's spiritual
domination at 1638–1639; the second coming of Christ at 1948; the
cleansing of the sanctuary, which would usher in a thousand years of
peace, at 2370–2436. White (1997) pointed out that Newton, "the
towering intellect, the pioneer and father of modern science, can now
stand alongside Newton the mystic, the emotionally desiccated obsessive and the self-proclaimed, but deluded, discoverer of the philosophers' stone – divested but undiminished" (p. 5). Likening Newton to
a mystic is resonant with some views of Wittgenstein.
Puritanism offered Newton a world of strict emotional and sensual

limits, where he did not have to find excuses for his inability to love. Rather, the twin pillars of God and knowledge replaced all other needs (White, 1997). His pious manner was mixed with an honesty commonly found in individuals with Asperger Syndrome. After years of squabbling between Newton and Leibniz over who had first discovered calculus, a committee was established to settle the dispute. Newton controlled the committee and even wrote its report, yet his fierce self-importance made him deny this later. It was a "rare blatant lie from Newton, the most pious of men," according to White (1997, p. 336).

Motor Clumsiness

There is no evidence that Newton had motor clumsiness. More than likely he had great fine-motor skills because of his adeptness at model making. His handwriting was very tiny; the implications of this are not clear.

Narcissism and Grandiosity

Newton showed many features of a narcissistic personality – grandiosity, hypersensitivity to other people's assessment of him, lack of empathy, difficulty in deriving satisfaction from his work, and interpersonal exploitation with arrogant or haughty behavior and attitudes. As mentioned, he was paranoid and constantly fearful of people stealing his work. He was also a hypochondriac, given to concocting remedies for himself and others. These characteristics are quite common in persons with Asperger Syndrome and genius.

Newton had grandiose ideas, particularly in terms of mythologizing his birth. That it occurred on Christmas day, along with the miraculous nature of his survival, held potent meaning for him.

Furthermore, his contribution to science was dependent on his service to God; indeed, his very vocation was to "unravel the laws governing God's universe" (White, 1997, pp. 64-65). This is close to views expressed by the mathematician Paul Erdös and Albert Einstein with respect to their work.

Newton showed a sense of entitlement to favorable treatment. For example, he sought a special dispensation from Charles II that would allow him to remain as professor at Cambridge but without taking holy orders as was required at the time. Again, this is not dissimilar to Wittgenstein's demands.

Mental Illness

Newton went through an episode of severe paranoid psychosis in 1693. It was temporary and believed to have been precipitated by the breakup of his intimate relationship with Fatio de Duillier. Nothing supports the view that it was chemically induced or work related. Newton wrote to Samuel Pepys, "I am extremely troubled at the embroilment I am in, and have neither ate or slept well this twelve month, nor have my former consistency of mind" (White, 1997, p. 247). While psychotic, Newton accused Locke of outlandish conduct: trying to "embroil me with women & by other means I was so much affected with it as that when one told me you were sickly & would not live I answered that it was better if you were dead" (White, 1997, p. 248). He recovered from the psychotic episode.

Originality of Thought

Newton's originality of thought marked his credentials as a genius. Newton was a complex and enigmatic genius. Gribbin noted that the essential feature of Newton's work is not what he did but the way he did it. The key point is that he invented what is now the scientific method, the idea of doing experiments to test theories and hypotheses (cited in Bragg, 1998). White (1997) claimed that Newton's great achievement was to clarify and to bring together the individual breakthroughs of men like Galileo, Descartes, and Kepler, and in doing so he produced a general overview – a set of laws and rules that has given modern physics a definite structure. Nonetheless, Newton's work demonstrates an extremely high level of mathematical creativity, which lies at the core of his genius.

Newton, in developing an intellectual foundation for science, stands in opposition to Wittgenstein, who adopted an anti-theoretical view of the world. Despite international recognition following the publication of the *Principia*, Newton felt that his life's work was unfinished. He continued to pursue a unified theory of matter until the final days of his life.

Newton's approach was to reduce everything to its simplest form, whether in science or biblical prophecy. The concept of simplicity was similarly espoused by Wittgenstein in his philosophy (Fitzgerald, 2004) and Einstein in his physics; as a framework it features strongly in the work of many geniuses.

Conclusion

There is no doubt that this complex and enigmatic genius was a perpetual loner, imposed extreme control on himself and others, and had the condition now called high-functioning autism or Asperger Syndrome. Newton was the greatest genius of the past one thousand years, and one can see the link between his psychopathological traits and his enormous creativity (Fitzgerald, 1999). His creative output was helped by his social detachment and his obsessive, driven approach to his work.

CHAPTER 3

Henry Cavendish
(1731–1810)

Henry Cavendish was a prominent English phys-icist and chemist, born in Nice to British parents. Having left Cambridge without a degree, he lived reclusively in London, devoting his life to scientific investigation while living on the fortune that he had inherited from an uncle. Cavendish discovered the composition of water and estimated the density of the earth – his value was within 1.5 percent of that attained by modern methods. He also estimated the density of the atmosphere, and studied electrical currents and astronomical instruments.

The English statesman William Cavendish, a first cousin of Henry and prime minister from 1756 to 1757, was described as having no intimate friends in political life: "This detachment was natural to him and inevitably confirmed his exalted station ... He was the supremely objective man, never led away by passion, completely reliable and so the ideal receiver of confidences ... Devoted to work and duty, everything the fourth duke did he did well" (Brown & Schweizer, 1982, p. 19). Jungnickel and McCormmach (1996) stated "these characteristics of the fourth duke – self-assured, conscientious, cautious, withdrawn, competent, and supremely objective – were those, by and large, of the Cavendish family and, in particular, of that member who distanced himself furthest for the active political life of the nation, Henry Cavendish" (p. 257). They also stated, "To judge from what we have seen, it would appear that he never recorded a feeling or a thought about life. He had a professional correspondence, which was never large but which is invaluable to his biographies, and a portion of this has survived" (Jungnickel & McCormmach, 1996, p. 5).

According to the engineer James Watt (1846), Cavendish was a rich man with a mean spirit. George Wilson (1851) defined Cavendish's universe as consisting solely of a multitude of objects that could be weighed, numbered, and measured, and characterized Cavendish as a calculating engine.

Possible Indicators of Asperger Syndrome

Social Behavior

Cavendish had "two rather forbidding traits ... a pathological fear of strangers that could render him speechless, and a clockwork regularity in all his transactions with life" (Jungnickel & McCormmach, 1996, p. 8). He was an extremely shy man.

"Like his namesakes in government, whatever Henry Cavendish did, he did well. Whatever he did not do well – which included delivering speeches, inspiring men to follow him into political battle, his special 'unfitness' – he did not do at all. He acted constantly in society, only his was not the given society of high fashion and politics, his birthright, but that of his own choosing, the society of scientific men" (Jungnickel & McCormmach, 1996, p. 257). Ordinary company caused him acute discomfort. Cavendish lived all his adult life in and around London in solid houses with servants to protect his privacy. These houses he turned into places of science, where the drama of his life was staged.

Narrow Interests/Obsessiveness

Cavendish's life was his science. Bickley (1911) pointed out, "There is something pathetic about such an existence as Henry Cavendish, so fruitful and yet so utterly barren" (p. 207). According to Edward Thorpe, general editor of Cavendish's *Scientific Papers*, Cavendish was not a man as other men are, but simply the personification and embodiment of a cold, unimpassioned intellectuality (see Note 5).

In a similar vein, Jungnickel and McCormmach (1996) stated, "Henry Cavendish existed in another world, though he may not have recognized it as a new world to conquer, one which demanded of Henry what had been demanded of the first duke, hard work. [By 'conquer' … we mean to understand the workings of nature, ruled by the authority of natural laws.]" (p. 10).

According to Jungnickel and McCormmach (1996), Henry had an interest in music, and made a mathematical study of it (on musical intervals): "Music was understood to be the art that spoke most directly to his feelings" (p. 127). The same could be said of Ludwig Wittgenstein.

Routines/Control

Cavendish had a clockwork regularity in all his transactions with life. The "move to Clapham Common was a particularly upsetting event in Cavendish's well-ordered life, but it could have been much worse. Cavendish, who in daily life always had held and depended on it, now had an associate, Blagden, who like his librarian was the soul of order" (Jungnickel & McCormmach, 1996, p. 238).

Cavendish had "demons that he could subdue only by imposing a vigilant orderliness on all phases of his life. By following in his father's footsteps, he brought his world together with that of science, with its discoverable orderliness, the calming paths of wondering stars, laid bare by nature, from which demons are strictly excluded. Cavendish left no 'inside narrative' of his life telling us why science attracted him, nor would we expect one from him" (Jungnickel & McCormmach, 1996, p. 368). Clearly he was reacting to the chaos that autism can create.

Language/Humor

As he was not good at delivering speeches, Cavendish avoided having to deliver them. Lord Brougham stated that he "uttered fewer words in the course of his life than any man who ever lived to fourscore years, not at all accepting the monks of La Trappe" (Jungnickel & McCormmach, 1996, p. 370). His silence was an acknowledgment of the inadequacy of customary spoken language to represent his world. When Cavendish did choose to speak, what he said was luminous and profound.

On the subjects he cared to speak about, Cavendish spoke precisely and sparingly as a point of conscience (Jungnickel & McCormmach, 1996). In fact, persons with high-functioning autism tend toward gravity (e.g., Ludwig Wittgenstein). Thomas Young stated that Cavendish's hesitancy of speech was not a physical defect but an expression of the constitution of his mind (see Note 6).

Lack of Empathy

Wilson, in his biography, according to Jungnickel and McCormmach (1996), "tried to penetrate to where Cavendish's courage, hope, and faith lie, his heart, only to discover that Cavendish was a "man without a heart"" (p. 8). Wilson described Cavendish as passionless, and said that he was only a cold, clear intelligence whose light brightened everything on which it fell, but warmed nothing. Berry (1960) noted Cavendish's "striking deficiencies as a human being" (p. 22). Indeed, his habitual profound withdrawal led one contemporary to characterize him as the "coldest and most indifferent of mortals" (Shapiro, 1991, p. 292).

Motor Clumsiness

A slouching walk was a family trait of the Cavendishes. Horace Walpole observed that a "peculiar awkwardness of gait is universally seen in them" (see Note 7).

Idiosyncrasies

According to Jungnickel and McCormmach (1996), the only portrait of Henry Cavendish is "a graphite and gray-wash sketch … Cavendish was an immensely wealthy man, but one would not know it from this portrait, which showed him in his rumpled coat and long wig, both long out of date, and with his slouching walk" (p. 8).

Conclusion

Jungnickel and McCormmach (1996) were probably on the point of diagnosing Cavendish as autistic, but for some reason stepped back from this position. They came extremely close, stating that Cavendish may have suffered from an affective disorder of a less familiar kind than depression. It is interesting that Jungnickel and McCormmach (1996) mentioned Newton and Einstein absolutely correctly in this discussion, but without using the word "autism." They refer to Cavendish's singular drive to understand the universe, and note that his mentality might one day invite a neurological and psychological interpretation. There is little doubt that he had an autistic desire to understand the world.

In the footnotes to their work, Jungnickel and McCormmach discussed Temple Grandin's (1986) autobiography. They pointed out that, regarding herself as a totally logical and scientific person and her autism as a disorder of affect and empathy, she recalls Cavendish in certain ways. Jungnickel and McCormmach observe in Cavendish a number of autisticlike traits: singlemindedness, apparent inability to feel certain emotions, secludedness, rigidities of behavior, odd gait, harsh voice, strange vocalizations, panic attacks, self-acknowledged social unfitness. There is little doubt that in hinting at autism they were absolutely correct.

Jungnickel and McCormmach are also correct in stating that Cavendish had access to an expression of feeling that was at once mathematically precise and distinct from the mathematics of natural description, one that could stand in for the spoken and otherwise conventionally acted out expression of feeling. These authors concluded: "This silent man is an endlessly fascinating figure ... when all is said and done, the person of Cavendish remains in large part in shadow. At the heart of the problem of Cavendish lies the mystery of human communication" (Jungnickel & McCormmach, 1996, p. 371). We feel that what he was demonstrating was high-functioning autism and the lack of a clear identity (i.e., part of his autism was a disorder of identity or identity diffusion).

CHAPTER 4

Thomas Jefferson
(1743–1826)

Thomas Jefferson, the third president of the United States and author of the Declaration of Independence, was a prominent revolutionary leader and political philosopher. The purpose of this chapter is to summarize the evidence that

Jefferson had Asperger Syndrome – a possibility that has already provided the subject matter of an entire book (see Ledgin, 2000).

Life History

Jefferson was born in Shadwell, Albemarle County, Virginia, on April 13, 1743. His father owned a plantation; his mother belonged to a prominent colonial family. He had read all his father's books by the age of 5 (McLaughlin, 1988). The young Jefferson was interested in various aspects of science and philosophy. He studied law, was admitted to the American Bar Association in 1767, and became a successful lawyer. He married Martha Wayles Skelton, a young and wealthy widow, in 1772. She died in 1782.

Jefferson was governor of Virginia from 1779 to 1781, and later in the 1780s was a minister of the U.S. government in France, where he witnessed the early stages of the French Revolution. As a representative of the Republican Party, he became U.S. vice president in 1797 and president in 1801. Jefferson officially retired from public life in 1809, but he continued to take a keen interest in the great issues of the day, such as slavery. He died on July 4, 1826 – 50 years to the day after the signing of the Declaration of Independence.

Possible Indicators of Asperger Syndrome

Social Behavior

Jefferson was extremely shy, socially awkward, and lacked empathy. Ledgin (2000) notes, "If anyone became emotional in his presence, he was likely to have been discomforted noticeably. If anyone raised his or her voice, almost certainly Jefferson would have found a polite way to remove himself" (p. 1). He failed to recognize social cues and was not very interested in other people. He also failed to recognize or understand irony and tended to be a concrete thinker and to lack common sense.

Ledgin (2000) speculated that Jefferson's relationship with Sally Hemmings (his wife's half-sister) was partly due to the fact that she was also an outsider, being a slave. Ledgin also pointed out that many people with autism spectrum disorders seek the company of others with similar problems, as in the case of Bertrand Russell and Ludwig Wittgenstein.

Jefferson's magnetic intellect made him interesting to others, and partly for that reason the one-sidedness of his conversations was tolerated, similarly to Wittgenstein's situation. Ledgin (2000) noted that Jefferson was apart from the mainstream in many respects and that he was eccentric and quirky.

Narrow Interests/Obsessiveness

Jefferson was described by James Parton, a nineteenth-century biographer, as a man who could "calculate an eclipse, survey an estate, tie an artery, plan an edifice, try a cause, break a horse, dance a minuet, and play a violin" (Ledgin, 2000, p. 195). His interests clearly were not narrow in the usual sense (they included architecture, birds, coinage, weights and measures, distance measurements, English prosody, grammar and etymology, Indian vocabularies, natural history, piano tuning, Philadelphia temperatures, and scientific phenomena), but he focused on each interest in a narrow and obsessive way. He spent extremely long periods of time writing and studying alone, and noted at the age of 75 that he was still a "hard student."

As U.S. president Jefferson established an economic embargo against England, which had devastating consequences similar to those of the Irish politician Eamon de Valera's economic war with Britain in the 20th century. He wrote an enormous number of letters, like Lewis Carroll (Fitzgerald, 2005) and many others with Asperger Syndrome. He spent 54 years constructing and reconstructing his home at Monticello.

Routines/Control

Jefferson favored ritual and preservation of sameness and tended to line up or carefully arrange books, works, or toys. From about 1767 onward, he formed a habit that developed into a daily ritual of "making memorandum book entries for the rest of his life. His recording of minutiae about expenditures evolved into an everyday exercise that served little if any purpose, for he lacked meaningful accounting abilities" (Ledgin, 2000, p. 28). For 60 or more years he started each day by soaking his feet in cold, preferably icy, water.

Temple Grandin (1986), an academic and author who has autism, says that Jefferson "compulsively measured the distance his carriage traveled" (Ledgin, 2000, p. 197). This is very similar to Tesla at the dining table and to some autistic mathematical prodigies. Ellis (1997) has noted that the computer would have been the perfect Jeffersonian instrument – for example, its impersonality would have suited him well.

Jefferson was extremely controlling, particularly in looking into every aspect of the University of Virginia, which he was involved in setting up. He was hopeless at managing his own finances and had massive debts when he died. According to Ledgin (2000), Jefferson's drawings for Monticello were carried out to precise scale and measured to several decimal places – the work of a compulsive personality.

Language/Humor

Jefferson was an extremely poor public speaker and avoided speaking in public as much as possible. Yet he had a great interest in English prosody – his kinds of linguistic interests are common in persons with Asperger Syndrome. It is noteworthy that his autobiography is unfinished. Persons with Asperger Syndrome have difficulty with autobiography.

Naivety/Childishness

Jefferson had a child-like personality and was emotionally immature. The great John Adams stated, albeit jokingly, "Jefferson was always a boy to me." Ledgin (2000) described him as utterly naïve, referred to an "Asperger's inclination to treat fiction as fact" (p. 70) and stated "his relative immaturity ... was what made him an either-or person, one who judged on the basis of perceived right or wrong without contingencies" (p. 72).

Nonverbal Communication

Jefferson was described as the "ever-elusive Virginian with the glacial exterior and almost eerie serenity" and had problems in expressing himself (Ellis, 2000, p. 74). His behavior was sometimes enigmatic and unpredictable. According to Ledgin (2000), "He had no talent for public speaking ... he seemed uneasy with eye contact. To some his body language appeared odd and awkward. He sang under his breath constantly. Often he looked disheveled, and he drank too much" (p. 1).

Ledgin (2000) listed the following features of autism in Jefferson: avoidance of eye contact in conversation, an inexpressive face or far-away look, few meaningful nonverbal gestures, failure to swing arms normally when walking, insensitivity to low pain levels, odd mannerisms, and trouble in starting conversation.

Jefferson was also described as having "limbs uncommonly long; his hands and feet very large, and his wrists of extraordinary size" (Chandler, 1994, pp. 26-27). His dress was extremely eccentric – he even wore slippers on state occasions. Further, Ledgin (2000) pointed out, "many of President Thomas Jefferson's close contemporaries would have believed his greeting guests accompanied by an uncaged mocking bird or with his hair in disarray were items not worth belaboring," as "polite people tend to look for and deal with the substance and character of those they admire" (p. 10).

Visual Thinking

According to Temple Grandin (1986), "There are two kinds of autistic-Asperger's thought. Some who are affected are visual thinkers like me, and others are numbers and word thinkers. Both types concentrate on the details instead of the overall concept. Visual thinkers like me and visual thinkers like Jefferson are good at building things and good at mechanical design. The nonvisual detail thinkers are good at accounting and mathematics. Both types have enormous memory" (cited in Ledgin, 2000, p. 204).

Jefferson was particularly interested in architecture. In 1786, he referred to his ability to think pictorially. He wrote of visualizing "architectural 'diagrams and crotchets' (jointed wood used as building supports)" as a means to relax in order to fall asleep (Ledgin, 2000, p. 43). Indeed, Monticello has been described as "the quintessential example of the autobiographical house" (Adams, 1983, p. 2). "Signs of that are everywhere, especially in the built-in gadgetry" (Ledgin, 2000, p. 88). This is reminiscent of Ludwig Wittgenstein's house in Vienna. Ledgin (2000) also stated that "architecture critic Paul Goldberger wrote that 'both conceptually and physically' the Jefferson intellect was central to the project. 'Jefferson's psyche' gave meaning to an exceptional architecture (Goldberger found in it 'nothing universal'), and the more deeply one might 'penetrate that psyche' the more pleasure one should draw from the place" (p. 88). According to Ledgin (2000), Jefferson "must be given credit for advancing America's household functionalism" (p. 91). Wittgenstein was also interested in functionalism.

It has been pointed out that for Jefferson, "beauty and function were inseparable" (Burstein, 1995, p. 21). This is exactly similar to Wittgenstein's ideas on architecture. Further, like Wittgenstein, Jefferson was an inventor.

Morality

Jefferson had, according to Ledgin (2000), an unyielding perception of right and wrong. He thought of the world in black and white. This is very characteristic of people with Asperger Syndrome. Ledgin (2000) also noted that "Jefferson ... made differing judgments about the worth of individuals on grounds of their ethical conduct, sometimes relying on only a few observations or experiences with them in order to do so" (p. 91). Wittgenstein may have made equally quick judgments based on insufficient information about people. We believe that this is because of the autistic condition.

Autistic Mental Mechanisms

Jefferson has been described as an "impenetrable man" (Peterson, 1970, p. viii). Ledgin (2000) notes, "Jefferson's knack for shielding himself against reality when fiction suited his romantic notions better," and that "Jefferson's taking of such poetic license influenced the drafting of the Declaration of Independence" (p. 20). This is similar to de Valera and the Irish constitution.

Ledgin (2000) also noted, "The biographer Ellis is probably the first among interpretative historians to discover that two levels of reality served Jefferson. Ellis wrote that Jefferson was capable of creating inside himself 'separate lines of communication' that would sort out conflicting signals. My Asperger's interpretation simply adds this: On the one hand there was reality as you and I know it, and on the other hand there was a Jefferson reality which the rest of us tend to see as idealism … The two levels are common to persons with high-functioning autism, and they deal with those separate realities daily in ways not yet clear to nonautistics" (p. 60). This is similar to de Valera's mode of operation (i.e., there was a "de Valera fact" and then there were facts recognized by persons without autism, or de Valera's autism – see Fitzgerald, 2004).

According to Ledgin (2000), Ellis noted that "denial mechanisms" gave Jefferson some guidance and that "interior defenses" protected him from becoming unduly pressed (p. 84). Ellis maintained that "capsules or compartments" had been "constructed" in Jefferson's "mind or soul" to stop conflicting thoughts from colliding (Ellis, 1997, pp. 88, 149, 174). Such compartmentalization is common in persons with autism, such as the artist L. S. Lowry; we also see it in Einstein (Fitzgerald, 2005).

In discussing high-functioning persons with autism, Ledgin (2000) stated, "To put it simply, they live mentally and perhaps emotionally on two planes. They live in our world of nonautistics, but they carry with them a separate and otherworldly 'reality' – *their* reality. The rest of us see it as idealism, but autistics seem to convert it into something palpable" (p. 58).

Conclusion

The evidence that Thomas Jefferson had Asperger Syndrome is very convincing indeed.

CHAPTER 5

Charles Babbage
(1792–1871)

According to Swade (2000), "The nineteenth century was not only an age of reason. It was also an age of quantification in which science and engineering set about reducing the world to number" (p. 12). It was thus a time when persons with high-functioning autism could come to the fore, and one such person was the English mathematician Charles Babbage.

Babbage spent most of his life trying to build calculating machines: first a "difference engine" and then a more ambitious "analytical engine." Astonishingly, the designs for the analytical engine "embody in their mechanical and logical detail just about every major principle of the modern digital computer" (Swade, 2000, p. 94). He is routinely referred to as the father, grandfather, forefather, great ancestor, or progenitor of the modern computer. He probably had autistic features but not the full syndrome of autism (i.e., PDD-NOS; pervasive developmental disorder-not otherwise specified).

Life History

Charles Babbage was born in Teignmouth, Devon, in 1792. He was an autodidactic mathematical prodigy – a precociously accomplished mathematician – when he entered Cambridge at the age of 18. There, "disaffected, independent-minded and even rebellious, he pursued a programme of study of his own which favored the works of French mathematicians. Babbage was a radical: He admired Napoleonic France" (Swade, 2000, p. 18). Many geniuses have been autodidacts.

Babbage described his father as "stern, inflexible and reserved, perfectly just ... never generous ... uncultivated except perhaps by an acquaintance with English literature and history," and said that he had no friend and was tyrannical (Swade, 2000, p. 22). Of note is the fact that the father suffered from extreme temper tantrums.

Babbage wrote first-class mathematical papers and clearly had an excellent mind. The Newtonian mind was an autistic mind. He wanted "the science of number (to) be mastered by mechanism. The 'unerring certainty' of mechanism would eliminate the risk of human error to which numerical calculation was so frustratingly prone" (Swade, 2000, p. 1). Infallible machines would compensate for the frailties of the human mind and extend its powers. No wonder persons with autism were attracted to this notion.

Babbage's attitude toward God was like that of many much later scientists. He was expelled from Cambridge because he proposed a thesis to prove that God was material. This thesis might have shown naivety and a lack of empathy; putting it forward certainly showed a complete disregard for the religious atmosphere of the university. It was self-destructive.

In 1821 Babbage was "happily married and enjoying the life of a gentleman philosopher in Regency London" (Swade, 2000, p. 25). Clearly this is not typically autistic. Only four of his eight children lived, and his wife died in 1827.

He became obsessed with developing a "calculating engine," about which he was very secretive. According to Swade (2000), he was "a fierce defender of moral probity" (p. 31).

Work

Babbage "was the great pioneer of computing and was equally famous on two counts – for inventing computers and for failing to build them" (Swade, 2000, p. 5). Babbage's engine stimulated the debate about the relationship between the mind and the physical mechanism of the brain. The notion that the machine was in some sense "thinking" was not lost on Babbage or his contemporaries. Harry Wilmore Buxton (1988), a younger contemporary of Babbage and his posthumous biographer, noted that Babbage had substituted brass and iron for the pulp and fiber of a brain, and had taught wheelwork to think, or at least to do the office of thought.

Babbage advocated for decimal currency, speculated about linking London and Liverpool by speaking-tubes, and foresaw the exhaustion of coal reserves and the role of tidal power as a source of energy. He kept scribbling books – something like Ludwig Wittgenstein's and the mathematician Paul Erdös's notebooks – that ran to between 6,000 and 7,000 sheets.

With monumental effort, he developed a new engine called the analytical engine, which could be programmed by the use of punch cards. According to Swade (2000), the conception and design of the analytical engine ranks as one of the most startling intellectual achievements of the nineteenth century.

In a way this machine describes autistic thinking – the mind of the person with autism is a kind of analytical engine mind. Babbage possibly did not have autism, but he was trying to develop an autistic thinking machine – which really is what a computer is and why persons with autism are so fascinated by computers. Nevertheless, the anthropomorphization of the computer mechanism as an autistic mind is problematical, given the subtlety and irreducibility of every human mind – autistic and nonautistic alike.

Later Ada Augusta Lovelace, the only legitimate daughter of the poet Byron, took an interest in Babbage's work. Lovelace herself might have had hyperkinetic syndrome; she certainly was quite narcissistic and regarded herself as a genius, which she was not. Nevertheless, she brought Babbage's analytical engine to the public attention.

Possible Indicators of Asperger Syndrome

Social Behavior

Babbage was "stubborn, determined, and convinced of the justice of [his] own position" (Swade, 2000, p. 61). He was a very sensitive personality. He married quickly without his father's approval and wrote to his friend John Herschel about the marriage without mentioning his wife's name. Herschel was shocked by the letter and said to him, "I am married and quarreled with my father – good God Babbage – how is it possible for a man to calmly sit down and pen those two sentences – add a few more which look like self-justification – and pass off to functional equations" (Swade, 2000, p. 21). This is a very autistic behavior.

Babbage was hypersensitive. George Airy, Astronomer Royal, stated that in relation to the calculating machine, "Mr. Babbage made the approval of the machine a personal question. In consequence of this, I, and I believe other persons, have carefully abstained for several years from alluding to it in his presence. I think it is likely that he lives in a sort of dream as to its utility" (Swade, 2000, p. 23).

"Babbage behaved as though being right entitled him to be rude, and the strength of his conviction tended to make him insensitive to the effect of his actions on others. These caustic public attacks were a shocking breach of the conventions of the day" (Swade, 2000, p. 63). He was called the "irascible genius" (see Note 8), was dominating and controlling, and had an "immoderate rage." His book "alienated the self-same people whose support he needed, and at the same time soured his relationship with the pre-eminent scientific body whose committees had three times recommended government support for his engine" (Swade, 2000, p. 64). He also had major arguments with his engine maker, Joseph Clement, which ended in total breakdown of the relationship, casting him in the role of *enfant terrible*.

Babbage worked in almost complete isolation. Maurice Wilkes, who studied his unpublished works, concluded, "Ever since going through Babbage's notebooks, I have been haunted by the thought of the loneliness of his intellectual life during the period when, as he later tells us, he was working 10 or 11 days on the Analytical Engine" (Swade, 2000, p. 226).

There was little doubt that Babbage had serious social relationship difficulties. When his 17-year-old son left for India, Babbage "took his farewell in the library, not troubling to see his son to the waiting cab. His indifference was not lost" on his son (Swade, 2000, p. 172). In some respects he had a fairly similar social life to that of the philosopher Immanuel Kant (Fitzgerald, 2005).

Nevertheless, Babbage became "a sought-after dinner guest. He was a celebrity, an engaging raconteur, full of wit and exuberant invention. To be able to say 'Mr. Babbage is coming to dinner' was the pleasure and delight of any hostess" (Swade, 2000, p. 73). Babbage was seen as a bon vivant with a love of dining out and socializing, and a good host and raconteur. With his brightly colored waistcoats, he was also something of a dandy. This is not typically autistic.

According to Swade (2000), Babbage at the age of 60 was "completely left out. Not just ignored, but actively excluded. His reputation for confrontation and protest as well as his earlier radicalism made him 'unclubbable'" (p. 185). This is quite autistic. Babbage tended to make himself an object of ridicule. In later life he "wrote pitifully of solitude and loneliness, and revealed the despair to which his efforts, personal sacrifices and lack of recognition had at times reduced him" (Swade, 2000, p. 190).

At his funeral there was only one carriage – that of the Duchess of Somerset – and few mourners. It would appear that both Babbage's genius and his failure might have been due to his high-functioning autism (if indeed he had this condition – the evidence is inconclusive). He failed in most professional relationships.

Narrow Interests/Obsessiveness

Swade (2000) noted, "The scope of his work was broad even by the generous standards of Victorian polymathy – mathematics, chess, lock-picking, taxation, life assurance, geology, politics, philosophy, electricity and magnetism" (p. 215). This is not typically autistic (although Thomas Jefferson also showed a wide range of interests and was almost certainly autistic). Nonetheless, Babbage became totally absorbed with his computing project by 1826, writing, "I did not pledge myself to devote my whole time exclusively to this project, yet I feel that the liberal and very handsome manner in which I was received at the Treasury would be but ill returned if I were to allow any other agreements to impede its progress. I have hitherto given up everything up for this object, situations far more lucrative … have been sacrificed, and I should not wish to change these sentiments now that it is approaching, I hope, to a successful termination" (Swade, 2000, p. 47). The machine was clearly an obsession for him.

According to Swade (2000), Babbage was "entirely seduced by the intellectual quest and propelled by an unremitting fascination with its mechanical realization" (p. 114). He "was driven by the exploration of the possible. He had glimpsed some profound vision, and he beckons to us over the heads of his contemporaries" (Swade, 2000, p. 117). He felt enormous satisfaction from the process of invention, which kept him so narrowly focused, stating, "I have given up all other pursuits for the sake of this" (Swade, 2000, p. 118). Swade also pointed out, "His pursuit of practical detail came not from any clear ambition to build the machine, but rather from his drive for the mastery of technique and the relish of the intellectual exploration of an extraordinary new world in which he was the first inhabitant" (p. 122).

According to Swade (2000), "Babbage was an inveterate inventor, and delighted in instruments, contrivances and mechanical novelties of all kinds" (p. 177). He was also interested in breaking ciphers and did succeed in breaking one. He had a great capacity to focus and to work – so great that, like Ludwig Wittgenstein and Isaac Newton, people worried about his sanity.

Routines/Control

Babbage was "a stickler for propriety and a fierce defender of moral probity"; he was always expressing "righteous indignation about issues that offended his sense of fairness" (Swade, 2000, p. 31).

Language/Humor

Babbage was a great storyteller, like Hans Christian Andersen and Arthur Conan Doyle (both of whom may have been autistic – see Fitzgerald, 2005). The geologist Charles Lyell stated in 1832, "We have had great fun in laughing at Babbage, who unconsciously jokes and reasons in high mathematics, talks of 'algebraic equation' of such a one's character in regard to the truth of his stories … I remarked that the paint on Fitton's house would not stand, on which Babbage said 'no, painting a house outside is calculating by the index of minus one,' or some such phrase, which made us stare; so that he said gravely by way of explanation, 'That is to say, I am assuming revenue to be a function.' All this without pedantry …" (Swade, 2000, p. 77). This type of thinking would typically reflect high-functioning autism.

Naivety/Childishness

Babbage set himself up as the "self-elected defender of the unwary by exposing scam, craft or infelicitous misrepresentation" (Swade, 2000, p. 50). When government funds ran out, he invested his own money in the project, which was naïve.

He wrote a very naïve book violently attacking the Royal Society, the premier scientific society of the day in England. He named people and made many accusations against them. This act seems hyperkinetic and impulsive.

He also mishandled his intervention with the Duke of Wellington, then foreign secretary. He was an extraordinarily poor communicator with politicians and frequently made major enemies. The fact that he talked to so few people about his engine probably interfered with its progress. The only place he presented it with great detail was at a meeting he held in Italy. He lacked diplomatic skills.

Anxiety/Depression

Babbage suffered from considerable depression at times, and tried to allay it with work. For example, he wrote *Passages from the Life of a Philosopher* while in a most distressed state. It reveals "practically nothing of his emotions or of the state of mind he was in when he set off from England" on a continental tour (Swade, 2000, p. 54). This is a kind of autistic style of autobiography. He was quite depressed in 1829, and wrote that he had suffered so severely in health that all his friends, especially the medical ones, were urging him to put his work to one side (Swade, 2000).

Mode of Thought

A scientist and administrator, Lyon Playfair stated, "Babbage was full of information" (Swade, 2000, p. 81). Swade pointed out that it was perhaps no accident that "Pascal and Leibniz in the seventeenth century, Babbage and George Boole in the nineteenth, and Alan Turing and John von Neumann in the twentieth – seminal figures in the history of computing – were all, among their other accomplishments, mathematicians, possessing a natural affinity for symbol, representation, abstraction and logic" (2000, p. 84). The relationship between the rules of logic and "laws of thought" tantalized the thinkers of Babbage's generation.

Idiosyncrasies

Eccentricity/esotericism. He was very sensitive to noise and organ grinders. He was an eccentric and comic figure. At the end of his life he "spoke as if he hated mankind in general, Englishmen in particular, and the English Government most of all" (Swade, 2000, p. 216).

Lack of common sense. Babbage had a great capacity for self-destruction and was headstrong. His lack of empathy and common sense was shown by the thesis he attempted to defend in the university (i.e., that God was a material agent). It was hardly surprising that he failed in this thesis, which was seen as blasphemous. This rebelliousness and lack of savoir-faire were to seriously impair his career.

Narcissism. Babbage was quite narcissistic and, according to Swade, "ached for recognition, titles and civil honors and growled at their lack." He was hardly likely to get these with the way that he criticized people (2000, p. 138).

Conclusion

It is possible that in Babbage we have a mathematician of genius who was not autistic, as there are signs both for and against. Against the notion of Asperger Syndrome was the fact that "at Cambridge he enjoyed student life to the full. He formed an enduring friendship with John Herschel … He played chess, took part in all-night sixpenny whist sessions, and bunked lectures and chapel to go sailing on the river with his chums" (Swade, 2000, p. 18). This does not sound like Asperger Syndrome. Some of Babbage's characteristics, such as his dandyism and love of socializing, would be more suggestive of hyperkinetic syndrome.

CHAPTER 6

Charles Darwin
(1809–1882)

Charles Robert Darwin was born in Shrewsbury on February 12, 1809, the fifth child of a wealthy family. He studied at Edinburgh and Cambridge, and in 1831, was recommended as an unpaid naturalist on the *HMS Beagle*, which was about to embark on a surveying expedition to South America. His studies on this voyage formed the basis for much of his later work on evolution and natural selection.

Darwin married his cousin Emma Wedgwood in 1839. They had 10 children, 3 of whom died in infancy. He lived in Kent, studying flora and fauna, and in 1859 published his magnum opus, *The Origin of Species by Means of Natural Selection*. He continued his studies despite ill health, and published many other works. He died on April 19, 1882, and was buried in Westminster Abbey.

This chapter explores the question: Did Darwin meet the criteria for Asperger Syndrome (Gillberg, 1991) or schizoid personality, or, indeed, was he simply a loner? (Wolff, 1995).

Family and Childhood

Darwin's paternal grandfather, Erasmus Darwin, was a well-known intellectual who was "as gifted in the field of literature as he was in science ... the archetypal gentleman polymath of his era." Darwin's maternal grandfather was the pottery magnate Josiah Wedgwood; both grandfathers were members of the Lunar Society, "a collection of wealthy men interested in machines and mechanical devices who met monthly at the time of the full moon" (White & Gribbin, 1995, p. 4).

Charles' father, Robert, was born in 1766. A "larger-than-life character," he had a large medical practice in Shrewsbury, and was "in turns kindly and severe" (White & Gribbin, 1995, pp. 5, 6). He married Susannah Wedgwood in 1796.

As a young boy Charles became a "great hoarder, collecting anything that captured his interest, from shells to rocks, insects to birds' eggs" (White & Gribbin, 1995, p. 6) and liked to go on long solitary walks (on one of which he was so deep in thought that he fell into a ditch) (Desmond & Moore, 1992).

His early childhood was a lonely time. On one occasion he beat a puppy because of the "sense of power it gave him" (White & Gribbin, 1995, p. 7). The death of his mother in 1817, when he was 8 years old, disturbed him greatly. His father became depressed and decreed that Susannah's death not be mentioned, so Charles had no opportunity to express his emotions on the matter.

One of Darwin's daughters, Elizabeth, may have shown signs of Asperger Syndrome. According to White and Gribbin (1995), "She never married and was content to live at home and to do odd jobs around the house and garden. A quiet and retiring child, she grew into a taciturn and reserved adult" (p. 237).

Possible Indicators of Asperger Syndrome

Social Behavior

As a child, Charles played solitary games in the vast family home. He was always something of a loner, and was noted to have an isolated, introspective nature. Young Charles detested the regimented learning of school; he would dash off afterwards and spend the evening at home, in his own room, although this was not allowed and he would have to run the mile back to school before locking-up time. His classmates regarded him as "old before his time and a very serious fellow" (White & Gribbin, 1995, p. 9).

Around his 30th birthday he considered marriage. "In his usual analytical fashion he drew up a list of pros and cons to assess the situation." He was concerned that "marriage would stifle him, prevent him from travelling if he decided he wanted to, that it would hinder his work by occupying too much of his time and that children might disturb his peace. It was an entirely selfish list of good and bad points, with scant concern for love or emotion; a purely scientific, pre-experimental treatment" (White & Gribbin, 1995, pp. 112–113). Despite his shyness and gentlemanly demeanor, he began to form a relationship with his cousin Emma Wedgwood, whom he had known since childhood.

Darwin was a great thinker, but had very little self-confidence. He was "a very humble man, totally dedicated to his studies, a scientist who worked meticulously and in solitude" (White & Gribbin, 1995, p. 2).

Narrow Interests/Obsessiveness

Throughout his life, Darwin was prone to obsession with particular living creatures. These included, at various times, orchids, beetles, barnacles, and earthworms. Science fascinated him from the age of 10. On holiday in 1819, he "spent most of each morning wandering off on his own to watch birds or to hunt for insects. Hours later he would return with specimens and spend the rest of the afternoon and early evening bent over his finds, devising methods of cataloguing them and trying to ascertain the species to which the various creatures belonged" (White & Gribbin, 1995, p. 10). He also spent hours poring over books about natural history in his father's library. After he and his brother Erasmus set up a science laboratory at their home, Charles was given the nickname "Gas" at school. He spent most of his allowance on buying the latest gadgetry and chemicals for his hobby, and continued with his experiments alone after Erasmus left for Cambridge. The brothers kept up a correspondence that was "full of chemical chat … leaving little room for comment on family matters" (White & Gribbin, 1995, p. 11).

In his teenage years, Charles "displayed an insatiable desire to kill birds of any variety … It was a peculiar obsession," according to White and Gribbin (1995, p. 12). He also liked to slaughter small animals, even though he was squeamish as a medical student and hated dissection. His father commented that he "cared for nothing but shooting, dogs, and rat-catching" and that he would "be a disgrace to himself and all his family" (White & Gribbin, 1995, p. 13). At Edinburgh University, he spent an inordinate amount of time reading the latest scientific, medical, and political literature. He frequently went off into the country from Edinburgh to collect specimens, neglecting his medical studies to follow his obsession. When he found a genuine interest, he would pursue it with an unmatched intensity.

At Edinburgh, Darwin began his life-long fascination with geology; while studying at Cambridge, he developed a "new obsessive fascination with entomology, and in particular, beetles" (White & Gribbin, 1995, p. 21). He then became very interested in botany. On the *Bea-*

gle expedition, he studied the wildlife of the Brazilian jungle and was particularly fascinated with the beetles and other insects living on the jungle floor. He began collecting fossil remains, made "detailed observations of flora and fauna and when he was not collecting wildlife, he doggedly hammered away at rock faces" (White & Gribbin, 1995, p. 62). The voyage lasted more than four years.

In 1846, Darwin started to study the barnacle, "a task which occupied almost all of his time for the next eight years" (White & Gribbin, 1995, p. 144). Although his health was bad, he had deliberately chosen to cut himself off from the world to concentrate on this arduous, tedious work, which involved using a microscope for hours at a time – each of his "beloved barnacles" was the size of a pinhead. He published four volumes on them, two describing living species and two describing fossil species. In the 1870s, he turned his attention to earthworms and the way they affect the environment, keeping thousands of them in jars in his study and greenhouse, and conducting experiment after experiment on them. He published a book and 15 scientific papers on earthworms.

In his autobiography, Darwin stated, "I think that I am superior to the common run of men in noticing things which easily escape attention, and in observing them carefully"; he also stated, "My habits are methodical" and referred to his "unbounded patience in long reflecting over any subject – industry in observing and collecting facts" (White & Gribbin, 1995, pp. 300–301).

Routines/Control

Darwin led his life in a highly organized fashion, rarely altering his routine. As the children began to leave home and Charles and Emma grew older, the pattern of their lives became even more mechanical and regulated.

During middle and old age, Darwin walked the same path almost every day on a strip of land near his house, surrounded by a gravel path. When he first formed the habit, he used to count the number of times he completed the circuit, kicking a flint onto the path at the end of each lap. It was on these walks that Darwin did most of his thinking: "Counting the laps and kicking the markers was all part of the mantra guiding the pattern of his thoughts" (White & Gribbin, 1995, pp. 259–260). Every night after dinner, Darwin played two games of backgammon with Emma. They kept a running score: At one point he was able to report that he had won 2,795 games while she had won only 2,490.

Darwin's extremely thorough and methodical cataloguing of his specimens might suggest an urge to establish control over the chaotic diversity of nature.

Language/Humor

There is no evidence that Darwin had problems in these areas. His writings are of a very high standard.

Lack of Empathy

Darwin's clinical views on the meaning of human existence and the primacy of "truth," as he saw it, made it difficult for him to be flexible or to compromise, even where the feelings of others were concerned. For example, he took a casual attitude to his own wedding. He appears to have regarded the ceremony as rather silly, showing little regard for the feelings of Emma or the two families. There was no proper reception; instead, he "whisked Emma off to the railway station with almost indecent haste and in so doing antagonized a number of relatives" (White & Gribbin, 1995, pp. 115–116).

Darwin "always had the habit of reducing everything to its fundamentals, of parrying all arguments with cold scientific logic" (White & Gribbin, 1995, p. 114). This made it difficult for Emma to explain her views on religion to him: She had to resort to writing him letters, in which she could pour her heart out and describe her feelings without clashing over meaning. In 1873, his method of writing to Huxley over some money that Huxley needed was more than a little clumsy, in Emma's opinion – further evidence of a lack of empathy.

Naivety/Childishness

Darwin was extremely slow to publish his theory of evolution and was unnecessarily cautious. While he delayed, the Welsh naturalist Alfred Russel Wallace came up with a similar theory. Darwin had been warned repeatedly that this could happen if he did not publish but apparently failed to perceive the danger.

Motor Skills

There is no evidence that Darwin had any difficulty in this area.

General Health

Darwin suffered from depression, especially after the death of his daughter Annie in 1851; he wrote to his colleague Joseph Hooker in 1875 expressing a "semi-serious desire to commit suicide" (White & Gribbin, 1995, p. 270). He was plagued by a succession of illnesses throughout the second half of his life: It was suggested that he suffered from multiple allergies and was hypersensitive to heat.

Conclusion

As far as Gillberg's (1996) criteria for Asperger Syndrome are concerned, Darwin does not meet the speech and language or the motor clumsiness criteria. However, according to Gillberg, motor clumsiness may be less a feature of high-IQ persons with Asperger Syndrome.

Neither abnormalities of speech and language nor motor clumsiness are necessary for a diagnosis of Asperger disorder under the *Diagnostic and Statistical Manual of Mental Disorders* (DSM-IV; American Psychiatric Association, 1994) classification; therefore, Darwin meets the criteria for Asperger disorder, which is broader in its definition than Gillberg's criteria.

Did Darwin have schizoid personality disorder? Though he had a detachment from social relationships, it was not pervasive, and he was a family man. Certainly, he chose solitary activities and took pleasure in these activities. He was not indifferent to criticism and did not show emotional coldness. Therefore, he did not meet the criteria for schizoid personality disorder, as defined by DSM-IV.

Did he meet the criteria for "loner" (schizoid personality) as defined by Wolff (1995, 1998)? He did demonstrate the following relevant features: social isolation and idiosyncratic behavior, high IQ, empathy problems, increased sensitivity, and single-minded pursuit of special interest. Ssucharewa (1926) noted that such persons tend to come from gifted families; Darwin's family was certainly gifted.

Regarding schizoid personality in childhood, Wolff (1998) noted that such children's special patterns were often sophisticated, quite unlike the simple, repetitive, stereotyped behaviors and utterances of autistic children. This applies to Darwin. Indeed, when Wolff followed up her loners, she found that two exceptionally gifted children – a musician and an astrophysicist – were able to transform their special interests into useful contributions to society, like Charles Darwin.

Family history studies are necessary to elucidate the link between Asperger disorder and schizoid personality. It is possible that great creative achievement, such as that of Darwin, is a much more difficult task without a capacity for solitariness and extraordinary focus on a specialized topic.

CHAPTER 7

Gregor Johann Mendel
(1822–1884)

The Austrian botanist Gregor Johann Mendel was a genius of the plodding, hard-working, single-minded sort – a genius for whom discovery was, as Thomas Edison put it, one percent inspiration and 99 percent perspiration. He was not a playful, intuitive genius like Picasso. (The great painter once said, "I do not seek – I find," an attitude that describes many of the men and women we now think of as geniuses.)

Mendel "toiled, almost obsessively, at what he did. But still he had that extra 1 percent, that inspiration that helped him see his results from a slightly different angle. It was this flash of insight that allowed Mendel to perform a feat of genius: to propose laws of inheritance that ultimately became the underpinning of the science of genetics" (Henig, 2001, p. 6).

According to Henig (2001) it was Mendel's non-heroism that allowed him to do the patient, thorough work through which his genius emerged (p. 168). A science was named in his honor: Mendelian genetics. High-functioning autism/Asperger Syndrome would be highly useful in this kind of plodding work, and this chapter presents the evidence that Mendel displayed this condition.

Mendel made the first tentative step towards a concept that would not be fully elucidated for another 50 years: the difference between phenotype (the way something looks) and genotype (the particular combination of genes that explains those looks) (Henig, 2001).

Life History

Mendel was born on July 22, 1822, near Udrau, in Austrian Silesia. His father, a farmer, did some experimental work with grafts to create better fruits. Mendel entered the Augustinian cloister at Brünn, and was ordained a priest. Having studied science at Vienna, he returned to Brünn and later became abbot. He studied plant variation, heredity, and evolution in the monastery's garden, particularly in pea plants. (It is interesting that many adults with autism work well in gardens; e.g., at Dunfirth in Ireland, people with autism live and work at activities such as organic vegetable growing that are intended to foster their growth and development.)

Mendel died at Brünn in January 1884, from Bright's disease (inflammation of the kidneys). Later, he was heralded as the father of genetics. During his years of anonymity, the priest was fond of telling his friends, "My time will come."

Work

According to Henig (2001), Mendel "observed that traits are inherited separately and that characteristics that seem to be lost in one generation may crop up again a generation or two later, never having been lost at all. He gave us a theoretical underpinning for this observation, too: he believed the traits passed from parent to offspring as discrete, individual units in a consistent, predictable, and mathematically precise manner" (p. 7). Sixty years after his death, a friend stated, "Not a soul believed his experiments were anything more than a pastime, and his theories anything more than the maunderings of a harmless putterer" (Henig, 2001, p. 164). During the winter, Mendel spent as much time as he could in the monastery library, doing meticulous work. His relationship to peas was probably similar to that of other persons with autism to numbers.

Possible Indicators of Asperger Syndrome

Social Behavior

Mendel was essentially homebound for his first forty years. In one photograph he is "standing in the precise middle of the group and looking off somewhere past the photographer's left shoulder" – he stands "erect and alone" (Henig, 2001, p. 121).

Mendel was a very shy person, with major peer and relationship problems. He had a naturally reticent personality: a friendly reserve with an underlying privacy. He was unable to do the most basic work that priests were required to do and was not in good health. He took to bed with a mysterious illness. Abbot Napp, the head of the monastery, stated that he was "seized by an unconquerable timidity when he has to visit a sick-bed or to see anyone ill or in pain. Indeed, this infirmity of his has made him dangerously ill" (Henig, 2001, p. 37).

When trying to do some teaching, he panicked and performed poorly at a teaching assessment that involved both an oral and a written examination. Professor Kanner, who examined his geological essay, described it as arid, obscure, and hazy, his thinking as erroneous, and his writing style as hyperbolic and inappropriate. Clearly Mendel had been an autodidact. Six years later he again tried to pass the certificate examination but panicked again and failed. According to Henig (2001), he was relegated for the rest of his career to the rank of uncertified substitute teacher.

Narrow Interests/Obsessiveness

As a boy Mendel was a disappointment to his father because of his reluctance to get out of bed. Mendel was attracted to book learning and joined the local monks.

Henig (2001) referred to a "one-track, simmering genius that had a chance to explode only years later, when the twin stars of intuition and accident were momentarily aligned in Mendel's favor, providing him an insight into the mystery of inheritance that few but he were prepared to understand" (p. 22). Henig thought that as a young man Mendel was probably eager, driven, and scientifically voracious. Nevertheless, he had interests other than experimental science: He became the official "weather watcher" for the city of Brünn and recorded meteorological readings every day. The fame that he longed for would come to him in his lifetime primarily as a local meteorologist. He was a skilled chess player (persons with autism are often interested in chess); he kept bees and gathered honey. He regarded his bees as his "dear little animals."

According to Henig:

> Mendel was also forever amusing himself with sci-
> entific and mathematical ideas that had nothing
> to do with plants. On the back of a draft of one of
> his dozens of church-tax missives, he scribbled lists
> that showed that, even in the midst of administra-
> tive tasks, he set himself new intellectual challenges.
> One of the most intriguing was a list of common
> surnames. Using several directories – the Military
> Year Book of 1877, the register of transporters, the

register of bankers, a barristers' year book – Mendel
collected more than seven hundred names, which he
arranged in different ways in an apparent attempt
to spot some sort of pattern. First he placed them in
alphabetical order, then he grouped them according
to meaning. (2001, p. 165)

Mendel's experimentation with peas was tedious work: In the autumn of 1857 alone, he had to shell, count, and sort by shape more than 7,000 peas, and that was just for one experiment, involving crosses between round and angular peas (Henig, 2001, p. 81). By the time he finished his work, seven years after he began, Mendel had conducted seven versions of this experiment, seven different monohybrid crosses, designed to look at plants that varied in only a single trait (shape first, then color, then height). By the time he had completed this succession of crosses, re-crosses, and backcrosses, he must have counted a total of more than 10,000 plants, 40,000 blossoms, and a staggering 300,000 peas. Virtually no one except a person with autism could do this.

Henig (2001) noted that Mendel applied his passion for counting almost indiscriminately to everything in his own little world. He counted not only peas but weather readings, students in his classes, and bottles of wine purchased for the monastery cellar. People with high-functioning autism are fascinated by numbers.

After Mendel became abbot of his monastery, he engaged in an obsessive letter-writing campaign against the new "monastery tax," which he continued until his death.

Routines/Control

"Monastery life was a balm to Mendel. Its regularity provided ease and comfort to a man who had spent his first twenty-one years in a thicket of uncertainty" (Henig, 2001, p. 25).

The orangery became his favorite place in the monastery. This is reminiscent of Ludwig Wittgenstein writing his philosophy in the warm botanic gardens in Dublin. He furnished the orangery with "a game table for playing chess; an oak writing table; six rush-bottomed nut wood chairs; and a few paintings. In his last years, when as abbot he could use the monastery's grandest rooms, he still spent his time in the orangery ... working through the mathematical, biological, and meteorological problems that vexed and intrigued him all the days of his life" (Henig, 2001, p. 65).

Language/Humor

Mendel, even to the end of his life, had a waggish and somewhat mischievous sense of humor, and "collected good jokes the way Darwin collected barnacles" (Henig, 2001, p. 163). He once upset the local bishop by saying, in what he thought was a whisper, that the bishop possessed "more fat than understanding." He would "walk slowly among the plants, which he liked to call his 'children' to get a reaction from visitors who did not know about his gardening experiments. 'Would you like to see my children?' the priest would ask. Their startled and embarrassed faces were always good for a chuckle" (Henig, 2001, p. 116).

Anxiety/Depression

Mendel became paranoid later in his life, just like Isaac Newton, and was suspicious of everyone, even his fellow monks, whom he thought to be "nothing but enemies, traitors and intriguers" (Henig, 2001, p. 162).

Mode of Thought

Mendel became interested in combination theory, which describes the relationship among the objects in a group arranged in any predetermined way. Henig (2001) saw this belief in combination theory as a mark of Mendel's genius: "Throughout history, some of the most creative minds have been those capable of maintaining two different mental constructs of the world simultaneously and applying the principles of one model to problems in the domain of the second" (p. 54).

The day he died, the local Natural Science Society heard a eulogy that referred to his "independent and special manner of reasoning" (Henig, 2001, p. 166).

Appearance

Henig (2001) quoted an acquaintance who described Mendel as "a man of medium height, broad-shouldered ... with a big head and a high forehead, his blue eyes twinkling in the friendliest fashion through his gold-rimmed glasses. Almost always he was dressed, not in priest robes, but in the plain clothes proper for a member of the Augustinian order acting as schoolmaster – tall hat; frock coat, usually rather too big for him; short trousers tucked into top-boots." His dress "bespoke his decorum and modesty; he was out in the world, but always a cleric" (p. 90). It is interesting that he is supposed to have had a big head: 50% of people with autism have big heads. This may be due to less pruning of cells early in life but may lead to a greater capacity to carry out mathematical calculations. When he walked, according to an acquaintance, he looked straight in front of him.

Conclusion

Mendel showed many of the criteria for Asperger Syndrome, particularly obsessiveness, social impairment, and love of routine. He also had the interest in counting, classifying, and mathematical calculation that is quite typical of the syndrome.

CHAPTER 8

Thomas "Stonewall" Jackson
(1824–1863)

The U.S. Confederate soldier Thomas "Stonewall" Jackson was born in Clarksburg, Virginia (which is now in West Virginia), on January 21, 1824, the third child of Jonathan Jackson, an attorney, and Julia Beckwith Neale. He was educated at the U.S. Military Academy at West Point and graduated in 1846, at which time he fought in the Mexican War. Due to ill health, he resigned from the army and lectured on military matters, but he entered the Confederate army on the outbreak of war in 1861. He soon earned his nickname, at the First Battle of Bull Run. As General Barnard E. Bee tried to rally his beleaguered men, he shouted to them: "Look! There is Jackson's brigade standing behind you like a stone wall!" (Douglas, 1940, p. 10).

Jackson showed himself to be a brilliant military strategist, often against larger Union armies. For example, his Stonewall Brigade distinguished itself in the Shenandoah Valley and at Richmond, the Second Battle of Bull Run, Harper's Ferry, Antietam, Fredericksburg, and Chancellorsville. At Chancellorsville he was accidentally shot by his own men; he died eight days later, on May 10, 1863.

Jackson studied war and military matters all his life, and was probably one of the greatest generals who ever commanded an American army. He was described as "a bold leader, probably the boldest the war produced" (Douglas, 1940, p. 62). Indeed, it was this boldness in unnecessarily visiting the front that led him to receive his fatal wound: an event that may well have lost the war for the southern states (Bevin, 1996). He was entirely indifferent to shells and bullets flying around him.

It appears that Stonewall Jackson meets the criteria for Asperger Syndrome, with clear evidence of a qualitative impairment in social interaction and restricted, repetitive, and stereotyped patterns of behavior, interests, and activities. Although individuals with Asperger Syndrome demonstrate major problems in social relationships, many are capable of great creativity because of their ability to focus on a single topic – in this case, on the field of battle and in military affairs. Jackson had "no moments of deplorable indecision and no occasion to lament the loss of golden opportunities" (Douglas, 1940, p. 62).

Family and Childhood

In 1826, Jackson's sister Elizabeth and his father died of typhoid; Julia Jackson gave birth to her fourth child, Laura, the day after her husband died. The family slid into poverty. Julia remarried; her new husband disliked the children and they were sent to live with relatives. Julia died in childbirth in 1831. Thomas's brother, Warren, died of tuberculosis in 1841.

Possible Indicators of Asperger Syndrome

Social Behavior

Jackson meets the criterion of a qualitative impairment in social relationships (American Psychiatric Association, 1994). He failed to develop peer relationships, and showed a lack of spontaneously seeking to share enjoyment and interests with other people, and of emotional reciprocity (Henry, 1979).

At school he was "shy and unsociable, retaining much … awkwardness" (Henry, 1979, p. 581). However, on the battlefield, he was extremely brave and disregarded his own safety; indeed, he was promoted on the battlefield for heroism.

After his first sight of Jackson at law school, Henry Kyd Douglas (author of *I Rode with Stonewall;* 1940) remarked to a classmate that Jackson was "such an oddity!" The classmate replied that "Old Jack is a character, genius, or just a little crazy. He lives quietly and don't meddle. He's as systematic as a multiplication table and as full of military as an arsenal. Stiff, you see, never laughs, but as kind hearted as a woman" (p. 233). ("Old Jack" was just 36 years of age at the time.)

Henry (1979) describes Jackson as "a withdrawn, morose, isolated personality of eccentric habits and with a hypochondriacal preoc-cupation which bordered on the bizarre" (p. 580). (Other individu-als thought to have shown Asperger Syndrome, such as Newton and the Austrian mathematician Kurt Gödel, were also hypochon-driacal.) During the Civil War, there were rumors that he was "mad," and some fellow officers resented his aloof, high-handed way of conducting his campaigns: "Like many another great soldier, he was at first called 'crazy,' but it was soon found out that he was always sober and in his right mind" (Douglas, 1940, p. 237).

The people of Lexington considered Jackson to be one of their local eccentrics, but despite his shyness and odd ways he was respected by members of his church. People considered his appearance odd, "and this, combined with his reserve and awkwardness in company, made him the object of many jokes and derisive comments" (Henry, 1979, p. 581). He had a shy, introverted and secretive personality and it has been said that he rarely if ever laughed.

According to Douglas (1940), Jackson "was not always in pleasant accord with officers next in rank to him and was apt to judge
them harshly" (this is reminiscent of Viscount Montgomery); "The
general always kept himself very much apart and, although he was
uniformly polite to all persons who came to see him, he did not encourage social calls" (p. 39).

Jackson never discussed his plans, and didn't offer advice to his superiors, nor ask it of his subordinates. He is reported to have said,
"If my coat knew what I intended to do, I'd take it off and throw it
away" (Douglas, 1940, p. 235). "This ignoring of the officers next in
rank to him detracted much from his personal popularity with them,
especially as he had no individual magnetism to attract them" (p. 47).
Nonetheless, his army "had unbounded confidence in their leader
and he in them" (p. 70), and "Never in the history of warfare has an
army shown more devotion to duty and the wishes of one man" (p.
135). Jackson judged himself more harshly than anyone else did.

Narrow Interests/Obsessiveness

Jackson was an avid reader of military history and studied Napoleon's campaigns intensively. He was capable of very intense, focused concentration. This extreme focus on a single topic can have
enormous benefits, and it is probably impossible for anyone to produce work of true genius without it.

Henry (1979) pointed out that Jackson was "hard working, personally brave and absolutely honest. He was also grim and humorless
and was noted for a remarkably single-minded, inflexible … persistence in any task he undertook" (p. 580). He "was not thought by

those who knew him best to be a good judge of character generally, yet his opinion of the generals opposing him was always wonderfully correct" (Douglas, 1940, p. 62). He was a brilliant strategist, described by an experienced federal officer as the "supremest flanker and rearer" the world had ever seen (Douglas, 1940, p. 220). In particular, he had a great ability to mystify, mislead, and surprise the enemy (Bevin, 1996).

Jackson was also preoccupied with religion and became a devotedly committed Christian of the stern, puritanical, biblical type. His difficulty with superiors was seen in 1850 when he was posted to Fort Meade in Florida. Before long, he was involved in an extraordinary and unpleasant dispute with his commanding officer, Major French. When Jackson accused French of immoral behavior, French counter-accused Jackson of insubordination. Here Jackson showed his "implacable and vindictive characteristics," and indeed his attack on French was "pitiless, narrow minded and legalistic" (Henry, 1979, p. 581).

Routines/Control

According to Douglas (1940), Jackson "seldom, if ever, complained, and never uselessly and apologetically to those under him, nor to those above him. Determined to deserve good fortune, he never quailed before disaster; but trusting in God, himself, and his army he always commanded success" (p. 34). Douglas continued, "He regulated his conduct, personal and military, in accordance with his own ideas of right and wrong; he acknowledged accountability to no one but God and his superior officers" (p. 35). He was incorrigible in disregarding his own ease and comfort.

A servant said that he "could always tell the military atmosphere by Jackson's devotions: that he didn't mind his daily prayers, but when he got up in the night to pray, 'Then I began to cook rations and pack up for there will be hell to pay in the morning'" (Douglas, 1940, p. 155). Douglas (1940) also noted that Jackson "read newspapers only for the facts they contained, when he read them at all. Their criticisms upon his movements or those of his associates he ignored. After a while he stopped reading them altogether" (p. 35).

Jackson remained "aloof and secretive and drove his soldiers mercilessly; and his discipline was almost inhuman but the troops marched and fought and died for him with remarkable devotion" (Henry, 1979, p. 584). His need for control was sometimes evident when he clashed with other officers, such as General Charles S. Winder.

Jackson could get by on five minutes of sleep snatched here and there: "He could sleep in any position, in a chair, under fire, or on horseback" (Douglas, 1940, p. 234).

Language/Humor

Jackson rarely laughed and talked very little. As we have seen, he was described as grim and humorless. We do not know whether he showed idiosyncratic use of words or repetitive patterns of speech.

Lack of Empathy

Douglas (1940) noted that General Jackson was always as hard as nails in the performance of a duty. Although he had a kind heart, he was inexorable in the execution of the law, and was never known to temper justice with mercy. Also, he always wanted to get rid of inefficient officers.

In one case early in the war, he did not allow an officer a short furlough to visit his dying wife, despite the man's impassioned appeal: "In cold, merciless tones, he replied, 'Man, man, do you love your wife more than your country?' and turned away. The wife died and that soldier never forgave Stonewall Jackson" (Douglas, 1940, p. 235).

At the Virginia Military Institute in Lexington, Jackson was a very bad teacher and extremely unpopular with his students. The cadets considered him a strange character: grim, aloof, unable to communicate with them in or outside the classroom, who subjected them to petty and relentless discipline (Henry, 1979). The authorities made an unsuccessful attempt to remove him from the job.

The general "had the least possible knowledge of music" (Douglas, 1940, p. 121). Henry (1979) reported an embarrassing incident when Jackson and his staff, as guests in a house, were being entertained by a young lady at the piano. Jackson asked her to play Dixie, saying that he thought it was very beautiful, whereupon the young lady replied that she had sung it just a few minutes earlier.

Naivety/Childishness

There does not appear to be much specific evidence for these traits in Jackson, but a few instances apply. He was shot at Chancellorsville after what Douglas (1940) described as an unnecessary visit to the front with a small number of his staff to investigate enemy movements – this would appear to be naïve behavior. In another example, he also showed reckless courage that even General Robert E. Lee thought excessive.

Nonverbal Communication

Jackson appears to have shown limited facial expression. He was "the worst-dressed, worst mounted, most faded and dingy-looking general" that anyone had ever surrendered to (Douglas, 1940, p. 162).

Douglas (1940) described Jackson's expression as "thoughtful, and, as a result I fancy of his long ill health … generally clouded with an air of fatigue … With high, broad, forehead, small sharp nose, thin, pallid lips generally tightly shut, deep-set eyes, dark, rusty beard, he was certainly not a handsome man" (p. 234).

While under fire, Jackson "rode along quietly, with his chin thrown out as usual and his cap close over his eyes, in apparent unconcern. I was wondering if this unconsciousness of the 'deadly imminent' shot flying through the air was simply indifference to danger, or the action of nerve and will-power; and this may have caused me, involuntarily, to imitate his bearing" (Douglas, 1940, p. 58).

Motor Skills

Jackson was ungainly: "in all his movements from riding a horse to handling a pen, the most awkward man in the army … He rode boldly and well, but not with ease or grace … He was not a man of style" (Douglas, 1940, p. 234).

Conclusion

There is no doubt that Stonewall Jackson met the criteria for Asperger Syndrome, which presents enormous challenges in terms of social relating and empathizing with others but can be hugely beneficial for a leader, as shown in this case. Stonewall Jackson was better prepared for the American Civil War than any other general.

CHAPTER 9

Gerard Manley Hopkins

(1844–1889)

The English poet and Jesuit priest Gerard Manley Hopkins was born in Stratford, Essex, on July 28, 1844. His father, Manley Hopkins, was a successful businessman with literary interests who wrote books on marine insurance and columns and criticism on a wide range of topics. His mother, Kate Smith, came from a wealthy London family; her father was a doctor near Tower Hill.

Hopkins was educated at High Gate School and at Balliol College, Oxford, and converted to Roman Catholicism in 1866, following John Henry Newman. He destroyed his existing poetry, became a Jesuit novice, and after studying for a period in Wales, taught in Sheffield and then at Stonyhurst School, Lancashire. He was ordained a priest in 1877.

Hopkins became professor of Greek at University College Dublin in 1884, and lived in Ireland for the remainder of his life. These were unhappy years for him, accentuated by his poor health. Norman White (1992) wrote, "Hopkins's powerful and original temperament, a strange mixture of innocence and expertise, of old prejudices and clear-sighted observations, worked against his achieving happiness and success" (p. vii). He died of typhoid on June 8, 1889, at the age of 44, and was buried in the same cemetery as the Irish patriots he so disliked.

Few of Hopkins's poems were published in his lifetime, but his work was anthologized after his death. The first edition, edited by his friend Robert Bridges, appeared in 1918 – and he became a highly respected and influential poet. He is known especially for the device of "sprung rhythm," whereby the numbers of syllables in lines may vary while the stresses remain the same. His best-known poems include "The Wreck of the *Deutschland*," "The Windhover," and "Pied Beauty."

Hopkins wrote, "I always knew in my heart Walt Whitman's mind to be more like my own than any other man's living" (White, 1992, p. 340). Whitman is thought to have had Asperger Syndrome; this chapter presents the evidence that Gerard Manley Hopkins may have had the same condition.

Family and Early Life

Hopkins wrote in 1878, "I do remember that I was a very conceited boy" (White, 1992, p. 1). He was the eldest of a large family. His mother was very interested in history; his father, Manley, wrote widely and showed features that we later see in Gerard, "the most obvious being voracity of mind" (White, 1992, p. 5). Besides books on aspects of marine insurance, Manley produced "two books of poetry, a drawing room play … a historical account of Hawaii, and, with his brother Marsland, a book of religious poems, differing from his other poetry" (White, 1992, p. 5), as well as book reviews, articles, dramatic monologues, hymns, letters, poems to newspapers, and an unpublished novel. His library included works on the orders of chivalry, rose growing, astronomy, and piquet, and he was interested in mathematical calculation – he appears to have had Asperger-type interests. In Manley's book *The Cardinal Numbers*, to which Gerard contributed, "facts become isolated from the argument in which they arise and, like the encyclopedic facts in Gerard's diaries, are marveled at in their own right" (White, 1992, p. 6).

Around the age of 10, Gerard "was precocious and original, and his aesthetic preferences were decided. When he and (his brother) Cyril had some childish illness his mother found him crying, 'because Cyril has become so ugly!' From an early age he showed a combination of inventiveness and didacticism, which were to become a characteristic of his poetry" (White, 1992, p. 19). He was also very interested in drawing and sketching, with an eye for detail, and was well known at school for his comic and grotesque drawings. However, he did not fulfill his early promise as a visual artist. He became very interested in architecture and was influenced by books on the Gothic style, whose values he became "dictatorial and priggish" in advocating (White, 1992, p. 21). He was always a close observer of nature – persons with Asperger Syndrome are often great observers (e.g., Gregor Mendel, Charles Darwin). A cousin remembered that as a boy in the garden, Gerard would arrange stones and twigs in patterns.

White (1992) noted, "He had a clear, sweet voice as a child but could not read music, and in spite of the family interest in music never learned to play an instrument properly" (p. 22). Later he tried to play and compose, and had to teach himself out of a textbook by trial and error. At 10 years of age he was "small for his age and delicate-looking, his head large in proportion to his trunk and shoulders. Photographs of him in the junior school show his mouth hanging open, eyes hooded, with the top lids heavy and half-closed … His eyebrows were already permanently raised, with an appearance of sardonic superiority" (White, 1992, p. 24).

Hopkins developed several friendships in his last years at High Gate. For example, he had a rather intense and intimate relationship with a boy named Alexander Strachey, but Strachey rejected him, which upset and baffled him greatly. He had an Asperger-style difficulty in negotiating relationships. Thus, it appears the reason Strachey did not go for walks with him was that Hopkins had not asked him. Hopkins hoped to learn from this relationship. White (1992) said, "There is an overwrought quality – as well as an innocence – about the account of an exchange with Strachey" that Hopkins recorded in great detail and sent to another friend, E. H. Coleridge. Hopkins and Strachey never made up; Hopkins commented to Coleridge, "It is still my misfortune to be fond of and yet despised by him" (p. 34). This type of communication problem often occurs in persons with Asperger Syndrome.

Hopkins did not really do well at school, and it was not a happy period for him. He could not negotiate the school relationships satisfactorily. However, university relationships are of a different quality, and he performed better there from a social interactional point of view. At the university for a time, he was nicknamed "Poppy," which may refer to his physique.

Possible Indicators of Asperger Syndrome

Social Behavior

For Hopkins, the Jesuits presented the most complete rational framework for resolving the problems of personality. Hopkins was hoping to impose on an unpredictable existence a sense of rightness and order, even at the price of putting himself out of joint, in some respects, with personal and national culture. In any event, his oddness and strangeness were merely exaggerated by his position as priest (White, 2002).

According to White (1992), "When the poems show an encounter between his private self and the outside social world it is seldom a happy one" (p. 381). Hopkins had major difficulties in behaving in socially appropriate ways. For example, while he lived in Dublin he was befriended by the McCabe family of Donnybrook, whom he often visited. One evening when taking his leave, he shook hands with McCabe and then held his hand out for the penny tram-fare (White, 2002).

In 1865, Hopkins wrote in a poem of "the incapable and cumbrous shame" that made him "more powerless than the blind or lame" in his dealings with other people. "His tendency was to find books more attractive than tutors; however authoritative he pretended to be, a book was a tool, which could be used as his impulse suggested" (White, 1992, p. 75). Solitude seemed preferable to him to company. In Dublin, 20 years later, he wrote, "To seem the stranger lies my lot, my life/Among strangers." The sense of being a stranger, of not fitting in, is common in people with Asperger Syndrome; this also reminds one of Temple Grandin's "anthropologist on Mars" metaphor.

In Dublin, Hopkins became known as "a small, shy, almost insignificant man" (White, 1992, p. 383) – he made little impact, and is hardly mentioned in the numerous Dublin memoirs of the time. It seems that he was soon forgotten in Ireland, and was invisible to Irish eyes. "In the classroom he was unable to cope with discipline, said a student, and never really won the confidence and affection of his pupils" (White, 1992, p. 385).

He was "twitted by his colleagues in the same sort of way as he was ragged by his pupils" (White, 1992, p. 385) – none of them intended to hurt him, and probably did not realize how sensitive he was. As a priest, he preferred his people to be unquestioningly devoted to authority, and therefore preferred to work with the poor in Lancashire rather than the educated and affluent in Oxford.

Hopkins had a harsh superego and was primarily homosexual – he "apparently never experienced guilt-free sexuality." He was scrupulous in detecting weaknesses of the flesh and "always anxious about the moral problems of physical beauty," whereas in fact "Nothing goes beyond glances, awareness, and 'temptations': the objects of attraction remain at a distance" (White, 1992, p. 114). Sexual "sins" were a major preoccupation; he would look up "dreadful words" in the dictionary. White (1992) commented, "When he gave up the idea of being a professional painter, because it placed too great a strain on his emotions, he was probably basing his decision on such temptations: 'evil thoughts' occurred to him while he was drawing, particularly when he drew a crucified arm, and a crucifix of his Aunt Kate's stimulated him in the wrong way" (p. 114). This suggests either sadism or masochism and excitement about it. According to White, "His reaction to his indiscriminate sexual feelings was a desire not to resolve but to crush them. His judgment by absolutes combined with sexual inexperience to produce a standard of female purity that was narrow even by the standards of the 1860s" (p. 129). White also pointed out the almost complete absence of women from Hopkins's writings, "except for virgin martyrs" (p. 164). He also felt guilty about idleness, inattention, lack of concentration, and spending time frivolously – just like Ludwig Wittgenstein, who had Asperger Syndrome (Fitzgerald, 2004). After a frivolous day Hopkins wrote, "Idling. Self-indulgence. Old habits [masturbation]. No lessons. Talking unwisely on evil subjects. Wasting time in going to bed." "By daily identification of short-comings, Hopkins hoped for self-improvement, but weaknesses continued to show themselves" (White, 1992, p. 119).

Hopkins was extremely scrupulous. He wrote "The Wreck of the *Deutschland*" having read in *The Times* about an incident in which a ship foundered in the mouth of the Thames, causing the death of some nuns who had been expelled from Prussia. He mentioned it to his rector, who said that someone ought to write a poem about it – so Hopkins did. It seems that "Particular aspects of this martyrdom appealed to him, and the event seemed to contain hidden messages and symbols: the German and English national implications, the reported cry of the tall nun, the number (five) of the nuns" (five being the number of Christ's wound's; White, 1992, p. 250). Hopkins appears to have been preoccupied with nuns.

Narrow Interests/Obsessiveness

"Hopkins's arrogance, reinforced by stubbornness, surfaced when he pursued one of his compulsive lines of interest. He had to choose his own questions, work out judgements according to his own rules and impulses, and find answers in his own time ... His obstinate independence of mind was constantly deflated by his recognition of areas of ignorance where he needed authority" (White, 1992, p. 75).

White (1992) also pointed out that Hopkins sometimes despaired at his apparent inability to control himself and his destiny. His solutions were typically impractical and extreme; his work was sometimes neurotically elaborate. He attempted to simplify his problems and evade his demons by complete submission to ancient comprehensive ideological systems; he became a Roman Catholic and then a Jesuit.

Hopkins was interested in linguistics and etymology, as persons with Asperger Syndrome often are. He became fluent in Latin and Greek. He frequently wrote about birds and animals – persons with Asperger Syndrome are often interested in nature. He was also fascinated by skyscrapers, as was Wittgenstein.

After more than a year in Dublin, "he had become not only more isolated but more intense and eccentric. Subjects which he could not argue about aroused an unbalanced dogmatism. Strange and disproportionate passions, not sanctioned by events, appear in his letters, and show why his reputation for eccentricity increased among the Irish" (White, 1992, p. 398).

For a period, Hopkins "bombarded his friend (Mowbray Baillie) with wild linguistic surmises, observations of obscure etymological coincidences, and demands for answers to questions on Egyptian language and mythology. Baillie had to expend midnight oil and patience to keep up with the constant letters and postcards – three were sent on one day" (White, 1992, p. 414). One wonders if Hopkins went through a mild hypomanic phase when he was doing this.

Routines/Control

Hopkins's social outlook was conservative. In Dublin, he was "indignant at the lack of respect his students showed him as a priest" (White, 1992, p. 17). He was suspicious of enjoyment, and, according to White (1992), frequently looked on beauty as a forbidden sweet, rather than as an essential of life.

Joining the Jesuits did not make much sense except as an Asperger-type decision: Indeed, it was a masochistic decision probably aimed at appeasing his cruel superego. The Jesuits' bodily penances of the time, which involved beating themselves, would somewhat appease the autistic superego and also give masochistic gratification.

Language/Humor

Hopkins was extremely interested in words, as we have seen. In his writings, he tended to use an elaborate, convoluted style of language, which could be seen as "Asperger language." Sometimes he sounds a "medieval note" . Persons with Asperger Syndrome, as they seem out of place or out of time, are often said to be like characters from the medieval or renaissance periods. This was true of the French avant-garde composer Erik Satie, for example (Fitzgerald, 2005).

There appears to be little evidence of Hopkins having a sense of humor apart from occasional practical jokes, such as blowing pepper with a bellows through a keyhole.

Lack of Empathy

Hopkins "never mentioned his father's job in letters, and showed no awareness that his comfortable home and education were dependent on his father's hard-won income and social position" (White, 1992, p. 5).

He was seldom tactful where art was concerned. In his assessments of his friends' work, he was more likely to blame than to praise, and to show insensitivity to personal feelings – this would be characteristic of someone with Asperger Syndrome. At his first meeting with the poet and critic Robert Bridges, who became his friend, Hopkins "crudely and uningratiatingly … tried to question the reserved Bridges on his morals, as though he were Bridges's parish priest," according to White (1992, p. 303). This was tactless.

Hopkins was a strong imperialist. While in Ireland, he was never able to put himself in the other person's position and look on Irish politics from an Irish point of view: The Irish sympathies he developed before he set foot in Ireland had narrowed or vanished (White, 2002). This would suggest a lack of balance and empathy.

Hopkins also showed his lack of empathy in an unintentionally amusing sermon he gave at supper in the community refectory in Wales one evening. The gospel of the day had been the feeding of the five thousand, and Hopkins took as his text the sentence "Then Jesus said: Make the men sit down." White (2002) suggested that he must have seen its ordinariness as a challenge to his powers of imaginative transformation and expansion. The sermon was not a success. After 15 minutes he had clarified neither argument nor purpose. He tried to rectify the situation by repeating the key phrase, *Make the men sit down.* Hopkins's voice was inclined to become shrill and lose authority when raised. His ineffective dramatization proved too much for the audience, and people laughed at it prodigiously. The last five minutes of the sermon were not delivered.

Naivety/Childishness

Hopkins never developed sexually and "never grew out of eccentric experimentation; after his death people remembered how as a Jesuit master he had shinned up a goal-post to cure a pupil's toothache, how he had rescued a monkey by climbing along a dangerous ledge" (White, 1992, p. 69). Persons with Asperger Syndrome tend to be novelty seeking in nonsocial situations.

Hopkins was always being misinterpreted. "He was 'so naïve and simple,' said John Howley, one of his students, that he 'neither suspected he was being ragged, [nor] was able to see that remarks of his were open to misreading.'" He once said that "he regretted that he had never seen a naked woman: this said in all simplicity opened up a new chance for ragging, and was perhaps even solemnly misunderstood" (White, 1992, p. 385).

While Hopkins was on a break in Monasterevin in Ireland, "On a long walk he was given a lift by a man in a cart. After some time he asked if they were now near Monasterevin; the reply was 'We're not, then, but we'll be coming into Portarlington presently.' Hopkins had not asked the man which way he was going, and they had been traveling in the opposite direction" (White, 1992, p. 495).

Hopkins showed "naïve emotional reactions" in political matters; for example, in his near-hatred of William Gladstone. He was a "naïve imperialist," according to White (1992, p. 157). While a Jesuit novice, in letters to his mother, he recounted with childish enthusiasm the injustices meted out to Catholics in Spain and Poland.

When he was studying in Wales, the older Jesuits regarded his enthusiasm for the Welsh language as naïve.

Moods

Hopkins suffered a great deal from depression; for example, June 1865 was a time of despondency and inertia when he could not get up in the morning or go to bed at night, and solitude seemed preferable to company. In 1885 he wrote,

> The melancholy I have all my life been subject to
> has become of late years not indeed more intense
> in its fits but rather more distributed, constant, and
> crippling. One, the lightest but a very inconvenient
> form of it, is daily anxiety about work to be done,
> which makes me break off or never finish all that
> lies outside that work. It is useless to write more
> than this: when I am at worst, though my judgment
> is never affected, my state is much like madness. I
> see no ground for thinking I shall ever get over it or
> even succeed in doing anything that is not forced on
> me to do of any consequence. (White, 1992, p. 394)

During a retreat in the Irish midlands in 1889, he said that he felt the loathing and hopelessness that he had often felt before. Fear of madness had made him give up the practice of meditating, except when on retreat. He complained a great deal in his letters, and showed a high level of self-pity. The Irish poet William Butler Yeats remembered him as "a sensitive, querulous scholar" (White, 1992, p. 425).

Identity Diffusion

During the second half of 1865, Hopkins thought he had passed through a crisis of identity. "The old self was repudiated, but he had not yet knitted together the valuable pieces of his past. It is doubtful if he ever achieved complete coherence – he seems always afraid of his unconquered demons, and took strong measures to keep them down ... Beneath the simple and apparently external form of Hopkins' apostasy lay a complex act of repudiation, involving an inability to come to terms with his own temperament" (White, 1992, p. 129).

It would appear that joining the Catholic Church was a way of trying to resolve his identity diffusion or confused identity. The Catholic Church was more rigid and therefore more attractive than the Anglican Church for someone lacking a strong core self. In another sort of identity confusion, White (1992) refers to clashes between Hopkins's poetic and priestly personae.

Appearance/Demeanor

In Dublin, many of his characteristics – appearance, way of talking, mannerisms, and so on – appeared typical facets of an English aesthete. Hopkins became known in Dublin as a small, shy, almost insignificant man; he was considered effeminate and stood out by, for example, wearing the kind of slippers that young girls wore at that time (White, 2002).

Conclusion

From the above, we feel that it is highly probable that Gerard Manley Hopkins had Asperger Syndrome.

CHAPTER 10

Nikola Tesla
(1856–1943)

The physicist, electrical engineer, and inventor Nikola Tesla was born into a Serb family in Smiljan, Croatia, at midnight on July 9, 1856. The family moved to Gospi when he was 6 years old, and he went to school there and in

Karlstadt (Karlovac). He then spent a year hiking in the mountains before attending the Austrian Polytechnic School in Graz. Financial difficulty forced him out during his second year, whereupon he went to Prague, where he seems to have taught himself in university libraries.

In 1881, Tesla got a job in the Central Telegraph Office in Budapest. While there he suffered a nervous breakdown and also conceived his revolutionary idea for an alternating-current motor. In 1882, he moved to Paris to work for Thomas Edison's Continental Edison Company, and in 1884, he immigrated to the United States, again to work for Edison.

Later he worked independently as an inventor, originating many important electromagnetic devices, including a transformer known as the Tesla coil. The standard international unit of magnetic flux density is called the tesla, in his honor. He became a U.S. citizen in 1891.

Nikola Tesla died in New York on January 7, 1943, at the age of 86. Eight months after his death, the U.S. Supreme Court ruled that he, and not the Italian physicist Guglielmo Marconi, was the inventor of the radio. His ashes were taken to Belgrade in 1957.

Tesla's biographer, Margaret Cheney (1981), described him as a modern Prometheus, and many have noted his gigantic impact on science, and thereby on human life in general. For example, the engineer B. A. Behrend stated, "Were we to seize and eliminate from our industrial world the results of Mr. Tesla's work, the wheels of industry would cease to turn, our electric cars and trains would stop, our towns would be dark, our mills would be dead and idle" (Cheney, 1981, p. 217). I.C.M. Brentano noted in Tesla's work "the importance of the achievements in themselves, as judged by their practical bearing; the logical clearness and purity of thought, with which the arguments are pursued and new results obtained; the vision and the inspiration, I should almost say the courage, of seeing remote things far ahead and so opening up new avenues to mankind" (Cheney, 1981, p. xvi).

While "people were to call him a wizard, a visionary, a prophet, a prodigal genius, and the greatest scientist of all time," some also defamed him as "a faker and a charlatan" and "an intellectual boa constrictor" (Cheney, 1981, p. 81). Some fellow scientists resented what they saw as his bragging to the press over his inventions. As Cheney (1981) pointed out, Tesla, "spending more time in his ivory tower than on ground floors, was to be smiled on fitfully by fame and in the long run ignored by fortune" (p. 183).

Family and Childhood

Tesla's parents were Milutin Tesla, a clergyman and spare-time poet, and Đuka Mandić. He claimed that he inherited his photographic memory and his inventive genius from his mother, who could recite verbatim whole volumes of native and classic European poetry.

Tesla began, when only a few years of age, to make original inventions: "When he was five, he built a small waterwheel quite unlike those he had seen in the countryside. It was smooth, without paddles, and yet it spun evenly in the current. Years later he was to recall this feat when designing his unique bladeless turbine" (Cheney, 1981, p. 7). He attempted as a child to fly with the aid of an umbrella, jumping off the roof of a barn and knocking himself unconscious.

Tesla had an experience in his village much like one that Ludwig Wittgenstein had at a later date in the mountains. The village had purchased a fire engine, and an attempt was made to pump water, but no water came. He "flung himself into the river and found, as he had suspected, that the hose had collapsed. He corrected the problem." Later he would recall, "Archimedes running naked through the streets of Syracuse did not make a greater impression than myself. I was carried on the shoulders and was the hero of the day" (Cheney, 1981, p. 7).

Possible Indicators of Asperger Syndrome

Social Behavior

Cheney (1981) notes that Tesla was "a loner by preference when the time for lone operators was swiftly passing" (p. 77), and as "a perennial bachelor, working apart, not entering into corporate associations, and not mixing with friends – his personal life was obscure to outsiders. Such reclusiveness [marked] the career of one of the world's leading figures in science and engineering" (p. xiii).

Although he was handsome and had a magnetic personality, Tesla was "quiet, almost shy" (Cheney, 1981, p. 79). Occultists and "odd men and women" were attracted to him, believing him to be "a man of prophecy and great psychic power who 'fell to Earth' to uplift ordinary mortals through the development of automation" (Cheney, 1981, p. 82). As he seemed indifferent to women in a sexual sense, there were whispers of homosexuality, but there was no evidence, and he appears to have been celibate. For a period in New York, he lived almost a hermit's existence. His friend Kenneth Swezey wrote, "Tesla's only marriage has been to his work and to the world, as was Newton's and Michelangelo's ... to a peculiar universality of thought. He believes, as Sir Francis Bacon did, that the most enduring works of achievement have come from childless men" (Swezey, 1927, p. 60).

In New York he was friendly with a couple named Robert and Katherine Johnston, who cultivated an elegant social circle, and often visited them. Katherine's letters to him suggest that she may have been in love with him. However, when Tesla "got around to responding," in typical Asperger fashion, his tone was inappropriately chiding: He "only succeeded in being cruel, going on about how he had found her sister, whom he had recently met, much more pretty and charming than she" (Cheney, 1981, p. 109). This is much like Ludwig Wittgenstein's reply to a woman who similarly had helped him (Fitzgerald, 2005).

Cheney (1981) described Tesla as a mutant or polymath: He was "part of no group or institution, he had no colleagues with whom to discuss work in progress, no formal, accessible repository for his research notes and papers. He worked not just in private but ... in secret." She pointed out that "the example set by Tesla has always been particularly inspiring to the lone runner" (p. 268).

The police regarded Tesla as a mad inventor. He showed sporadic anti-Semitism.

Narrow Interests/Obsessiveness

In his youth, Tesla's favorite pastime was reading: He would read until dawn. He said that in his teenage years, his "compulsion to finish everything, once started, almost killed him when he began reading the works of Voltaire. To his dismay he learned that there were close to one hundred volumes in small print ... But there could be no peace for Tesla till he had read them all" (Cheney, 1981, p. 18).

Regarding his method of invention, Tesla wrote, "I do not rush into actual work. When I get an idea I start at once building it up in my imagination. I change the construction, make improvements and operate the device in my mind. It is absolutely immaterial to me whether I run my turbine in my thought or test it in my shop. *I even note if it is out of balance*" (emphasis in original; 1919, p. 12).

Cheney (1981) noted that Tesla reported another curious phenomenon that is familiar to many creative people – that there always came a moment when he was not concentrating but when he *knew* he had the answer, even though it had not yet materialized. "And the wonderful thing is," he said, "that if I do feel this way, *then I know I have really solved the problem and shall get what I am after*" (emphasis in original; p. 14).

At the Polytechnic School in Graz, Tesla brashly suggested to his physics professor that a particular direct-current apparatus would be improved by switching to alternating current. The professor responded that this was an impossible idea, but instinct told Tesla that the answer already lay somewhere in his mind. He knew he would be unable to rest until he had found the solution. (In fact, he wrote in his usual flamboyant way that it was a sacred vow, a question of life and death. He knew that he would perish if he failed (Cheney, 1981). Years later, as he was walking in a city park with a friend, the solution came like a flash of lightning. He had hit upon a new scientific principle of stunning simplicity and utility: the principle of the rotating magnetic field produced by two or more alternating currents out of step with each other (Cheney, 1981).

Tesla himself acknowledged, "I do not think there is any thrill that can go through the human heart like that felt by the inventor as he sees some creation of the brain unfolding to success ... Such emotions make a man forget food, sleep, friends, love, everything" (Cheney, 1981, p. 107). In relation to marriage, he stated, "an inventor has so intense a nature with so much in it of wild, passionate quality, that in giving himself to a woman he might love, he would give everything, and so take everything from his chosen field. I do not think you can name many great inventions that have been made by married men" (Cheney, 1981, p. 107).

Like Edison, Tesla could work without sleep for two to three days. In the later part of his life, he took a great interest in pigeons. Indeed, an entire chapter of Cheney's biography is entitled "Pigeons." He regarded them as his sincere friends. According to Cheney (1981), "No one knew when the inventor began gathering up the sick and wounded pigeons and carrying them back to his hotel," where he took care of them (p. 187).

Tesla told a strange story to John J. O'Neill (his first biographer) and another writer, as recounted by Cheney (1981). He said that he had fed thousands of pigeons over a period of years but that there was a special white pigeon – the joy of his life – that he loved as a man loves a woman, and that loved him and lent purpose to his life. When she was ill, he stayed beside her for days and nursed her back to health. Tesla said that finally, when the pigeon was dying, she came to see him and a blinding light came from her eyes. When she died, something went out of his life, and he knew that he would not complete his work.

Tesla wrote poetry but never published it, considering it too personal. He could recite poetry in English, French, German, and Italian.

Cheney (1981) noted that Tesla "threw out all accessories, including gloves, after a very few wearings. Jewelry he never wore and felt strongly about as a result of his phobias" (p. 79). He was afraid of germs and fastidious in the extreme.

Routines/Control

In his 30s, when he dined at the Waldorf-Astoria Hotel in New York, Tesla followed a remarkable routine as illustrated in the following: "Eighteen clean linen napkins were stacked as usual at his place. Nikola Tesla could no more have said why he favored numbers divisible by three than why he had a morbid fear of germs or, for that matter, why he was beset by any of the multitude of other strange obsessions that plagued his life. Abstractedly he began to polish the already sparkling silver and crystal, taking up and discarding one square of linen after another until a small starched mountain had risen on the serving table. Then, as each dish arrived, he compulsively calculated its cubic contents before lifting a bite to his lips. Otherwise there could be no joy in eating" (Cheney, 1981, p. 1).

Tesla feared being controlled by others but could be very controlling; for example, of his secretaries. Cheney (1981) noted that he subjected himself at a very early age to iron discipline in order to excel. He wrote that up to the age of 8, his character was weak and vacillating, but a book by a Hungarian novelist somehow awakened his dormant powers of will, and he began to practice self-control.

As a young man, he started to gamble on cards and games of billiards. However, he was able to conquer this passion. Later in life he smoked heavily and drank coffee to excess but once again used his willpower to stop completely. It would be unusual for someone to do this as successfully as he did.

Language/Humor

Tesla spoke in a shrill, high-pitched, almost falsetto voice. Franklin Chester stated, "When he talks you listen. You do not know what he is saying, but it enthralls you … He speaks the perfect English of a highly educated foreigner, without accent and with precision … He speaks eight languages equally well" (Cheney, 1981, p. 78). He does not appear to have had a developed sense of humor.

Lack of Empathy

The young Tesla developed two concepts that would later be important to him: that human beings could be adequately understood as "meat machines," and that machines could, for all practical purposes, be made human. Cheney notes, "The first idea may have done nothing to improve his sociability, but the second was to lead him deep into the strange world of what he called 'teleautomatics' or robotry" (p. 15). Thirty years later, he marveled at the unfathomable mystery of the mind.

Tesla displayed occasional streaks of cruelty: People with Asperger Syndrome often have aggression in them. In an interview that he gave to *Collier's* magazine in 1926, Tesla described a future ideal society modeled on that of the beehive, with desexualized armies of workers whose sole aim and happiness in life would be hard work (Cheney, 1981).

Tesla was interested in eugenics. George Viereck (a German immigrant and friend of Tesla, who was later imprisoned for disseminating pro-Nazi propaganda) reported Tesla as saying that in a harsher time, survival of the fittest had weeded out less desirable strains, and proposing sterilization of the "unfit" in order to preserve civilization and the race. (Cheney, 1981, observed that one cannot say to what extent these sentiments originated with Tesla as opposed to Viereck.)

Naivety/Childishness

Tesla sometimes showed what might be interpreted as typical Asperger naivety in his business dealings. Soon after he started to work for Edison, he proposed a plan to make Edison's dynamos work more efficiently – a major job. Edison responded, "There's fifty thousand dollars in it for you – if you can do it." Tesla's salary was $18 per week at the time. Tesla worked flat out for months and succeeded in making the promised improvements, but when he asked for the fifty thousand dollars, Edison told him, "you don't understand our American sense of humor." When Tesla threatened to resign, Edison offered him a $10 per week raise (Cheney, 1981, p. 33).

When George Westinghouse said that his company could not continue to exist if it paid Tesla his full royalties, Tesla trusted him and tore up his contract. Thus, according to Cheney (1981), Tesla "not only relinquished his claim to millions of dollars in already earned royalties but to all that would have accrued in the future. In the industrial milieu of that or any other time it was an act of unprecedented generosity if not foolhardiness" (p. 49). He should have been a fabulously rich man based on his inventions, but in later life he had financial difficulties that even hindered his research.

In 1916, Tesla was summoned to Court to pay $935 to the city of New York in personal taxes. Cheney (1981) noted that the misfortune seemed unjustly cruel, coming at a time when Edison, Marconi, Westinghouse, General Electric, and thousands of lesser firms were thriving on the profits from Tesla's patents. Tesla was penniless and swamped by debts and was even in danger of imprisonment.

The novelist Julian Hawthorne (only son of Nathaniel Hawthorne) described Tesla as having "the simplicity and integrity of a child" (Cheney, 1981, p. 78).

Nonverbal Communication

During his blockbuster lectures in the United States and Europe in 1891 and 1892, Tesla was "a weird, stork-like figure on the lecture platform" (Cheney, 1981, p. 51), yet he was handsome, and had a tremendously powerful personality. His hands were large and his thumbs abnormally long. "He was too tall and slender to pose as the physical Adonis, but his other qualifications more than compensated." His eyes were "like balls of fire" (Cheney, 1981, p. 79).

Motor Skills

Tesla does not appear to have been clumsy or awkward, given his dexterity as an engineer and his almost professionally skillful billiard playing.

Comorbidity

Tesla appears to have manifested signs of mental and physical comorbidity in many phases of his life. For example, he experienced a "strange partial amnesia" at the start of the 1890s, and "was shocked to discover that he could visualize no scenes from his past except those of earliest infancy" (Cheney, 1981, p. 62).

In about 1881, he had a nervous breakdown during which he could hear the ticking of a watch from three rooms away. "A fly lighting on a table in his room caused a dull thud in his ear. A carriage passing a few miles away seemed to shake his whole body. A train whistle twenty miles distant made the chair on which he sat vibrate so strongly that the pain became unbearable. The ground under his feet was constantly trembling" (Cheney, 1981, p. 21). During this period his pulse fluctuated wildly, and his flesh twitched and trembled continuously. Yet his health returned, and soon after he solved the problem of the alternating-current motor that had been plaguing him for years.

As a child, Tesla contracted malaria and cholera; in his 60s, he was troubled by strange illnesses from time to time.

Conclusion

Like Charles Darwin, Stonewall Jackson, and John Broadus Watson, Nikola Tesla appears to have met the criteria for a diagnosis of Asperger's disorder, which is defined more widely than Asperger Syndrome. Neither abnormalities of speech and language nor motor clumsiness are necessary for Asperger's disorder under the American Psychiatric Association (1994) classification.

CHAPTER 11

David Hilbert
(1862–1943)

T he German mathematician David Hilbert was born in Königsberg on January 23, 1862. He studied and taught at Königsberg University until he transferred to the University of Göttingen in 1895, where he made an immense contribution to various fields of mathematics. For example, in 1900, he proposed 23 mathematical problems for investigation, most of which have since been solved.

Hilbert was described as a gay young man with a reputation as a snappy dancer and a charmer who flirted outrageously with a great number of women – traits that would not suggest Asperger Syndrome. However, this chapter will present evidence that he may in fact have displayed characteristics of this syndrome.

Life History

Richard Courant found Hilbert to be "a unique personality, profoundly immersed in his work and totally dedicated to his science, a teacher and leader of the very highest order, inspiring and most generous, tireless and persistent in all of his efforts" (Reid, 1970, p. 2). His mother Maria Therese was an unusual woman – she was interested in philosophy and astronomy, and fascinated by prime numbers. His father was a county judge, "rather narrow in his point of view with strict ideas about proper behavior, a man so set in his ways that he walked the same path every day and so rooted in Königsberg that he left it only for his annual vacation on the Baltic" (Reid, 1970, p. 3).

As a boy, Hilbert had an intense desire for truth, but he described himself as a dull and silly youth. He found memorization exceedingly difficult, and language classes caused him more sorrow than joy. He was not particularly quick at comprehending new ideas. A member of the Hilbert family recalled, "all I know of uncle David is that his whole family considered him a bit off his head. His mother wrote his school essays for him. On the other hand, he could explain mathematics problems to his teachers. Nobody really understood him at home" (Reid, 1970, p. 6). Mathematics appealed to him, and he was delighted with it because it was easy and effortless. It required no memorization.

Hilbert found the perfect mate, married, and fathered a child in 1893. The boy, Franz Hilbert, was "disturbed." Hilbert said "I must consider myself as not having a son" (Reid, 1970, p. 139; Einstein also ignored a son with mental illness). It is not clear whether or not Franz had schizophrenia, but he did announce that he wanted to save the family from evil spirits that were after them. It was said that he lacked tact and would speak of his views inappropriately.

Work

Hilbert did not grasp complicated ideas in a flash and took his time to get to the bottom of matters. He set high standards of simplicity and clarity for his talks to the mathematics club. After his death, *Nature* described Hilbert as a "mathematical Alexander." This is typical of persons with Asperger Syndrome and genius; there is a parallel with Wittgenstein.

Hilbert's conception of mathematical existence was freedom from contradiction. He divided his working life into periods during which he occupied himself almost exclusively with one particular problem. If he was engrossed in integral equations, integral equations seemed everything. When he dropped a subject, he dropped it for good and turned to something else. There were five periods in his working life:

1. theory of invariance (1885–1893)
2. theory of algebraic number fields (1893–1898)
3. foundations – (a) of geometry (1898–1902); (b) of mathematics in general (1922–1930)
4. integral equations (1902–1912)
5. physics (1910–1922).

Max Von Lau, a Nobel Prize winner, noted, "Pure mathematics … did not fail to impress me, especially in the brilliant courses of David Hilbert." He went on to say that Hilbert was "the greatest genius I ever laid eyes on" (Reid, 1970, p. 68).

Hilbert's lectures were in some ways like Wittgenstein's, in that he prepared them only in the general sense and then tried to work out the details in the lecture. At times they were mathematics in the making. His lectures were a faithful reflection of his spirit (direct, intense).

Possible Indicators of Asperger Syndrome

Social Behavior

For Hilbert, comradeship and human solidarity were essential to scientific production (contrary to an Asperger trait). He complained about a lack of mathematical conversation. Students had to be careful about offering a lie or an empty phrase to him, and his directness could be something to be afraid of (Reid, 1970, p. 53). He was not good with children.

Hilbert was described as "a bit of an arrested juvenile" (Reid, 1970, p. 131). He would come to a lecture hall in short-sleeved open-necked shirt – inconceivably inappropriate attire for a professor in that day. He pedaled through the streets with bouquets from his garden for his "flames," but was just as likely to bear as his gift a basket of compost balanced on the handlebars. At a concert or restaurant, no matter how elegant, if he felt a draught, he borrowed a fur or a feather boa from one of the ladies present. He liked pretty young ladies and delighted in explaining mathematical ideas to them. He fancied himself a dashing man of the world.

Hilbert thought the war was stupid, and said so (not unlike Bertrand Russell's views). He refused to sign a declaration in favor of the war and was treated as a traitor.

Narrow Interests/Obsessiveness

Hilbert had an extraordinarily focused attention on mathematics – he once described himself as a mathematical Eskimo. Richard Courant said that Hilbert had "a fantastic balance between intense concentration and complete relaxation" (Reid, 1970, p. 109).

Routines/Control

As we have seen, Hilbert imposed strict self-control in terms of work. He was also controlling of others; when he went to a restaurant after a lecture, the subject of conversation was "only algebraic number fields" (Reid, 1970, p. 51). His active influence on the mathematicians of his time was embodied in a statement that one of them made directly to him: "You have made us all think only that which you would have us think" (Reid, 1970, p. 214).

He absolutely denied the reality of his physical illness – pernicious anemia – which was more or less fatal at the time he got it. It seems that his wife was entirely devoted to him and looked after him. However, there is no sense of reciprocal social interaction with her. She simply provided for all his needs, while he was totally controlling, dominant, and he appears to have entirely imposed his will on her in the home situation. He would have been lost without her and could not have lived the life he lived.

An example of the importance of routines in Hilbert's life appears in an anecdote told about him: One day, at a party in their house, his wife asked him to go upstairs and put on a clean shirt. After some time, when he had failed to reappear, she went upstairs and found him asleep in bed. For Hilbert, the natural sequence of things was to take off his coat, then his tie, then his shirt, and so on, and then go to sleep (Reid, 1970).

Language/Humor

Hilbert delivered his lectures with many repetitions to make sure that everyone understood him and repeated briefly what had been covered in a previous lecture. His sentences followed each other simply, naturally, and logically. We have no definite evidence of abnormalities in this area. What was very unusual about his language was its content, with an almost exclusive focus on mathematics.

Naivety/Childishness

Hilbert was said to have had "all the naivety and the freedom from bias and tradition which is characteristic only of true great investigators" (Reid, 1970, p. 53). His mathematical approach was to go back to questions in their original conceptual simplicity. George Polya said that Hilbert always "looked so innocent" (Reid, 1970, p. 132).

Hilbert demonstrated a "naïve and imperative egoism" that was always "egoism in the interest of his mission, never of his own person." He once made an interesting comment about Einstein: "Do you know why Einstein said the most original and profound things about space and time in our generation? Because he had learned nothing at all about the philosophy and mathematics of time and space" (clearly, he thought spending too much time reading others' work was counterproductive) (Reid, 1970, pp. 141–142).

Lack of Empathy

Alfred North Whitehead wrote, "The leading characteristic of mathematics is that it deals with properties and ideas which are applicable to things just because they are things, and apart from any particular feelings, or emotions, or sensations, in any way connected with them. This is what is meant by calling mathematics an abstract science" (Whitehead, 1948, p. 2). It is perhaps one of the reasons why the study of mathematics has attracted many people with Asperger Syndrome.

Hilbert seemed to lack tact in his relationship with "the flames" he pursued. He basically denied the existence of his son when he got ill. He couldn't really relate to children, as we have seen, and would spend just a minute or so with them. This is not unlike Bertrand Russell.

While he had very intense relationships with mathematicians, these were exclusively focused on discussing mathematics, which is typical of Asperger Syndrome. He could also relate in a social way to students, but again, even at dinner, mathematics was the focus. The brutality with which he could dispose of someone who did not meet his standards was well known. Hilbert once told Norbert Wiener, later a famous mathematician himself, that his lecture was "the worst there ever has been!" (Reid, 1970, p. 170).

Despite being married himself, Hilbert was against scientists marrying. When Wilhelm Ackerman married, Hilbert was very angry and refused to do anything more to further Ackerman's career. Ackerman, a gifted young logician, had to teach in a high school.

Nonverbal Communication Problems

From photographs, Hilbert appears to have had a peculiar, stiff gaze.

Motor Clumsiness

He was probably not clumsy because he was a good dancer. In very high-IQ Asperger Syndrome, clumsiness does not come into the picture. It is possible that in cases where clumsiness does come in, a somewhat lower IQ exists and maybe more severe brain pathology. (True Asperger Syndrome probably does not include clumsiness, which should therefore be excluded as a criterion for it – this may be the one item that Asperger himself got wrong.)

Anxiety/Depression

In 1908, Hilbert became depressed and spent time at a sanatorium. The breakdown did not seem to be triggered by any specific experience. Courant, in the Foreword to Reid's (1970) book, wrote that "almost every great scientist I have known has been subject to such deep depressions." He felt that this might be due to periods in the life of a productive person when he appears to himself to be losing his powers, which can come as a great shock.

Conclusion

David Hilbert meets the criteria for Asperger Syndrome, according to Gillberg (1996), with the exception of an absence of speech and language problems and motor clumsiness. However, neither of these features is essential for such a diagnosis, while their absence would suggest a diagnosis of Asperger's disorder under the American Psychiatric Association (1994) classification. It is likely that Asperger Syndrome/disorder helped Hilbert to become as creative as he was in mathematics because it gave him the kind of exclusive focus that is necessary for major creativity.

CHAPTER 12

H. G. Wells
(1866–1946)

The prolific British writer Herbert George Wells, who is known particularly as a pioneer of science fiction, was born in Bromley, Kent, on September 21, 1866, the son of a shopkeeper. He was educated at the Normal School of Science in London, and, having been a draper's apprentice for a time, held various jobs before becoming a full-time writer in 1895.

Wells was a deep and idealistic thinker on society and the individual's role within it; for a time he was a member of the left-wing Fabian Society, whose members included George Bernard Shaw. Wells tended to be argumentative, and he fell out bitterly with Shaw and others.

In 1890, Wells married his first cousin, Isabel; they were soon divorced. He married Amy ("Jane") Robbins in 1895, and had numerous affairs, including a 10-year relationship with the writer Rebecca West, which produced a son, Anthony.

Wells's works in the science-fiction genre include *The Time Machine*, *The Island of Doctor Moreau*, *The Invisible Man*, and *The War of the Worlds* – all of which, along with much other writing, he produced in a burst of productivity in the second half of the 1890s. More conventional novels included *Kipps* and *The History of Mr. Polly*; he also wrote non-fiction, including the hugely popular *The Outline of History*. In all, he produced more than 100 books in a 50-year writing career. He developed an interest in world government, social planning, and ways of controlling technology for the benefit of society. He had a massive prophetic imagination, exemplified in his prediction (see Note 9) of "the Age of Motors, down to a detailed description of sweeping throughways, the congestion in city centres and the suburbanisation of the countryside" (MacKenzie & MacKenzie, 1973, p. 163).

H. G. Wells died on August 13, 1946, six weeks before his 80th birthday. He was an enigmatic character – the contention of this chapter is that his idiosyncrasies are best explained by the presence of Asperger Syndrome.

Family and Early Life

Wells's father, Joseph Wells, was the son of a gardener. While he acquired a love of plants, he somehow failed to acquire the disciplines of his trade – he was restless, given to spurts of enthusiasm, impatient to the point of being quick-tempered, and had a taste for being his own master. He was also quick-tempered and irritable; he may have shown signs of a combination of Asperger Syndrome and hyperkinetic syndrome. He had a great liking for books but was a poor manager of his life. In 1853, he married H. G.'s mother, Sarah Neal, an innkeeper's daughter with an ingrained evangelical view of the world (MacKenzie & MacKenzie, 1973).

Soon after the birth of the first child, Frances, Joe Wells lost his job as a gardener. When he was offered another post, he refused. This was a disastrous decision. The couple took over a china shop in Bromley from a cousin of Joe. This shop never did well; Joe supplemented their income as a semi-professional cricketer. The marriage was an unhappy one, with a high level of conflict and intimacy problems. Sarah suffered from depression and Joe "failed as a husband and father" (MacKenzie & MacKenzie, 1973, p. 15), possibly because of his Asperger Syndrome. He was generally happier when he was away from Sarah's moans about his inadequacy. Sarah became pious and self-pitying; she was prone to snobbery and regretted the fact that Joe was not a gentleman.

Three further children were born: Frank in 1857, Fred in 1862, and H. G. ("Bertie") in 1866. Frances died in 1864, to her mother's great distress; Bertie was seen, in a way, as a substitute. Joe developed "a slow but profound estrangement from all the values his wife was determined to uphold. Sarah was too rigid in her outlook, too stereotyped in her beliefs, for a husband who enjoyed small talk and whiling away his evenings with cards and draughts" (MacKenzie & MacKenzie, 1973, p. 19).

As a baby, H. G. was cross and tiresome, according to his mother. Asperger babies are often like this. As a child he was precocious and good at drawing. He was very controlling and would not share his toys, and like his father, he suffered tantrums. H. G. later wrote, "I made a terrific fuss if my toys or games were touched and I displayed great vigor in acquiring their [his brothers'] more attractive possessions. I bit and scratched my brothers and I kicked their shins" (MacKenzie & MacKenzie, 1973, p. 21). Frank, the oldest boy, was a rebel, who found neither a cause nor a niche, ending up as an itinerant clock repairer. H. G. described him as a complete failure in life, like his father.

When H. G. was 7 years old, his leg was broken in an accident – one of the luckiest events of his life, as he described it in his autobiography (Wells, 1934). During his weeks of recuperation, he was exposed to a wide range of books and developed a great interest in reading, which opened the world to him. As a child, H. G. "roamed around Bromley, sometimes alone." He was a very observant boy (persons with Asperger Syndrome are often great observers).

Wells stated that at the end of his childhood he had been "a senti-mentalist, a moralist, a patriot, a racist, a great general in dreamland, a member of a secret society, an immortal figure in history, an im-pulsive fork thrower, and a bawling self-righteous kicker of domes-tic shins" – "a dress-rehearsal for much of his adult life" (MacKenzie & MacKenzie, 1973, p. 30).

His first job was as an apprentice in a drapery shop. He performed poorly and was dismissed. As a young person, the books he most admired were Tom Paine's *Common Sense*, Swift's *Gulliver's Travels*, and above all, Plato's *Republic*. MacKenzie and MacKenzie (1973) noted that these represent three themes – "radicalism and agnosti-cism, utopian satire, and the idea of a rational society ruled by men of intellect – which played a predominant role in his ideas and his writings" (p. 39). By the age of 14, he had acquired autodidactic habits of learning that remained with him all his life – curiosity, impatience, "a bubbling excitement at discovering facts or making connections that were already known to the better-educated, and a passionate belief in the power of words to stir the imagination" (MacKenzie & MacKenzie, 1973, p. 40). Novelty seeking and a fas-cination with words are characteristic of Asperger Syndrome.

At the Normal School of Science in South Kensington, Wells "not only absorbed (T. H.) Huxley's pessimistic gloss on evolutionary theory, but he was also affected by the work of Kelvin and oth-ers who insisted that the law of entropy would eventually lead to a cooling of the sun and the reduction of the planets to a system of dead matter whirling in the nothingness of space" (MacKenzie & MacKenzie, 1973, p. 120). Wells left the college "with wilted qualifications and a reputation as an inattentive and undisciplined student. The dream that he might make a career as a scientist was shattered" (MacKenzie & MacKenzie, 1973, p. 69).

After suffering a few serious illnesses, of which the exact nature is not known, he gained a first-class honors degree in zoology from the University of London, having taken a correspondence course, and also became a Fellow of the College of Preceptors. At this time he was working as a teacher of science. He appears to have been a good and successful teacher and wrote a biology textbook. He had a superego and was conscientious and untiringly helpful to his students. One of his pupils later described him as showing "evident signs of poverty, or at least disregarding any outward appearance of affluence. In dress, speech and manner he was plain and unvarnished, abrupt and direct, with a somewhat cynical and outspoken scorn of the easy luxurious life of those who have obtained preferment and advantage by reason of social position or wealth ... he was extremely painstaking" (MacKenzie & MacKenzie, 1973, p. 83).

Work

Wells started to publish stories in periodicals around 1895, the year of his divorce. They were very well received – the *Review of Reviews* described him as a man of genius. He was employed as a theater critic by the *Pall Mall Gazette*, but, according to MacKenzie and MacKenzie (1973), he "never had much sense of the theatre, nor did contemporary stage versions of his tales have much success. Though he hugely enjoyed charades and amateur theatricals, he could never catch the peculiar quality of illusion which must be fused in a play" (p. 109). This may have been because of his Asperger Syndrome.

He badgered his publishers: "He was … intensely suspicious, and one or two small instances of sharp practice confirmed his view that any unwatched publisher might well swindle him of his due. The result was that Wells was always in the market, and no publisher could ever be sure that he would have the next book, or on what terms he would get it; and even when a contract was signed he could expect a steady flow of criticism of his shortcomings and attempts to tell him how to run his business" (MacKenzie & MacKenzie, 1973, p. 112). Persons with Asperger Syndrome tend to be rather paranoid, controlling, unempathic, and intrusive.

Wells's work was compared with that of Jules Verne, a comparison that both men disavowed on the basis that Verne's work was more scientific. Wells "always wrote as a moralist, concerned with man's place among the mysteries of Nature, or the social implications of mastering them. Verne reflected mid-century optimism about progress, celebrated the advance of science, and conscientiously tried to work out what marvels might lie on the hidden agenda of the future. The similarity of their subject matter obscured this contrast between the pessimist and the positivist" (MacKenzie & MacKenzie, 1973, p. 118). Wells produced stories that were rich in symbolism and dreamlike in their structure: It is not true that persons with Asperger Syndrome cannot use symbolism, as is often thought.

"Several of the stories … used the theme of *doppelganger* – the idea of double identity. In 'The Late Mr. Elvesham,' 'The Stolen Body' and 'The Plattner Story' Wells revealed his fascination with the idea of dual personality which breaks out repeatedly in his later fiction" (MacKenzie & MacKenzie, 1973, p. 118). Persons with Asperger Syndrome often feel split and certainly have identity diffusion. Wells used models of writing that "matched his own psychic preoccupations (such as the feeling of double identity or the alienation of the outsider) or his cosmic obsessions (such as the nature of man and the fate of his planet)" (MacKenzie & MacKenzie, 1973, p. 119). His writing embodies a sense of impending apocalypse.

The Island of Doctor Moreau describes the agony of beasts made half-human by surgery. The study of nature, according to Moreau, "makes a man at last as remorseless as nature." Man "is still only half a human being, a creature torn between its mental aspirations and its instinctual drives, and thereby condemned to unending pain and torment. In case the analogy between Moreau's beasts and normal man had been missed, Wells underlined it. After the final horrors on the island after Moreau's death, the beast-men begin to regress. Prendrick, the scientist who has been cast away on the island, manages to escape and returns to London. There he looks at the 'blank expressionless faces of people on trains and omnibuses,' and fears that 'they would presently begin to revert, to show first this bestial mark and then that'" (MacKenzie & MacKenzie, 1973, p. 125). Here he may be describing certain Asperger-type experiences.

In *The War of the Worlds*, "anything weak or silly" will be wiped out by the Martians' heat-rays as their tripods stalk on through the blackened ruins toward London. In this deeply pessimistic story, Wells wrote that only "able-bodied, clean-minded men" would survive: men who would obey orders and ensure the future of an untainted race by mating with "able-bodied, clean-minded mothers and teachers" (p. 128). This reminds one of the writings of George Orwell, who also had Asperger Syndrome (Fitzgerald, 2005).

Around the turn of the century, there was some criticism of "the disproportionate realism that almost amounted to vulgarity" in Wells's books (MacKenzie & MacKenzie, 1973, p. 152). For example, Edward Garnett wrote, "the author as artist has not so completely absorbed & assimilated the author's philosophy" as to conquer "the rather hard prosaic exact creed of *explanation, analysis and demonstration*": Wells had been so involved in recording his personal life that he had failed to realize that "life is so much greater than any possible *explanation* of it" (MacKenzie & MacKenzie, 1973, p. 122; emphasis in original). Because Wells could not distinguish between life and art, he had begun "to justify his inability to distinguish [them] into a principle." This difficulty of distinguishing life from art is a classic Asperger issue. Virginia Woolf was later to attack Wells for disinterest in the mental and emotional life of his characters and for the detailed realism of his novels. What else can a writer with Asperger Syndrome do?

MacKenzie and MacKenzie (1973) note that in Wells's later novels, the autobiographical theme was used as a substitute for self-revelation, rather than as a means to it. "Wells indulged himself in his past, relying on his power of vivid description and good story-telling to obscure the fact that he was unable to use his experience at the emotional level required to transmute life into art. He drew upon his own life for plot and detail like a reporter rather than a novelist, setting the scene brilliantly but failing to people it with characters that were anything more than comic caricatures, puppets for his ideas, or projections of himself. At each point where his larger designs required him to transcend the obvious, to explore behind the self-image of which he made such free use in his fiction, some emotional inhibition frustrated him" (p. 280).

This is a critical observation, because it is a classical Asperger style of writing. Henry James wrote of "the co-existence of so much talent with so little art, so much life with (so to speak) so little living!" but found Wells "more interesting by his faults than he will probably ever manage to be in any other way" (MacKenzie & MacKenzie, 1973, p. 282). Again, this is a typical comment about an Asperger person.

Possible Indicators of Asperger Syndrome

Social Behavior

In school, Wells had one friend, an older and more sophisticated student. It is typical of persons with Asperger Syndrome to have a single good friend – often older. Many of his friendships were carried out largely by correspondence, which would suit the Asperger person. He drew comic sketches in his letters. Persons with Asperger Syndrome can form loyal, long-lasting relationships. There is usually a highly intellectual element to the relationships, which tend to be with fellow intellectuals or fellow thinkers.

When Wells was working as a teacher, he "had already acquired a knack of using his acquaintances as sounding-boards for whatever fancy was quick in his mind" (MacKenzie & MacKenzie, 1973, p. 48) – this is reminiscent of Ludwig Wittgenstein. At college he was "bewitched" by the evolutionist T. H. Huxley; he "remained so, emotionally and intellectually, to the end of his days" (MacKenzie & MacKenzie, 1973, p. 57).

In the debating society at college, Wells loved smashing popular beliefs and was a great talker, which is common in persons with Asperger Syndrome. He was a gawky student and socially insecure. His first wife, Isabel, was shy and simple. During their courtship he "talked to her, and at her" (the "at" is typical Asperger Syndrome). She had to listen to his rambling discussions of "atheism and agnosticism, of republicanism, of the social revolution, of the releasing power of art, of Malthusianism, of free love and such-like liberating topics" (MacKenzie & MacKenzie, 1973, p. 67) – topics in which she had no interest, as she was unintellectual and conservative by nature. This is typical of a one-way Asperger kind of discussion.

In the marriage, "He did not realize that the drive to subjugate Isabel crushed whatever chance there might have been that she could grow to meet him on more equal terms" (MacKenzie & MacKenzie, 1973, p. 88). He was showing the Asperger Syndrome over-control here. The pattern of a typical Asperger marriage started to develop; he "began to keep his interests to himself, especially when he found that even conversation on petty topics died or escalated into irritable tiffs" (MacKenzie & MacKenzie, 1973, p. 89). Wells discovered that his ideal was an illusion now that Isabel was his wife.

Once he was married, he felt trapped – he found marriage a prison and wanted to get out of it. Early in the marriage he seduced one of Isabel's friends. Infidelity then became a feature of his life. Wells became attracted to a student of his named Amy Robbins (known then as Catherine). His abstract idea of the ideal woman, Venus Urania, "had failed to embody herself in Isabel ... My mind was seizing upon Amy Catherine Robbins to make her the triumphant rival of that elusive goddess ... in her turn, I was trying to impose a role" (MacKenzie & MacKenzie, 1973, p. 92). Many Asperger marriages break down.

His language in a letter to Robbins regarding an attack of illness – "When we made our small jokes on Wednesday afternoon about the possible courses a shy man desperate at the imminence of a party might adopt, we did not realize that the Great Arch Humorist also meant to have his joke in the matter" (p. 93) – is reminiscent of the type of language used by Paul Erdös, a mathematician with Asperger Syndrome.

In 1891, Wells had a meeting with Frank Harris, editor of the *Fortnightly Review*, about an article that Wells had written. The meeting did not go well because Wells, instead of explaining the article to Harris, who did not understand it, concentrated on the state of his top hat – he had dressed up for the meeting, but "couldn't for a moment adopt the tone and style of a bright young man of science. There was my hat tacitly revealing the sort of chap I was." When he got home Wells smashed the hat – "the symbol of a failure which hurt him so much that he claimed he could not attempt another serious article for a year or more" (MacKenzie & MacKenzie, 1973, p. 87). This is a good example of problems that persons with Asperger Syndrome have in interpersonal relationships. What Harris wanted was not high-flown abstractions but vivid metaphors that would illuminate for his readers the new and strange, and even terrifying, world into which science was carrying them. But because of his Asperger Syndrome, Wells was tending toward high-flown abstractions.

Wells and Isabel parted in early 1894, over his relationship with Ms. Robbins; he and Catherine eloped together. It seems that no strong sexual passion was driving them together – Wells wrote of "immense secret disillusionments" – but Catherine was quick, amusing, and more sophisticated than Isabel. MacKenzie and MacKenzie (1973) observed that Wells had abandoned a wife whom he had been unable to subjugate, and chosen a mistress who was willing to live her life through him and for him.

In being willing to live her life through and for Wells (just as David Hilbert's wife did for him, for example), Catherine was the ideal "Asperger wife." They married in 1895. After experimenting with various nicknames for her, he settled on Jane. At this time, Wells was "uneasy in company, unsure of his manners and given to shyness. He knew he lacked polish. He had a very high-pitched voice, between a husky squeak and a falsetto, and something of a cockney accent. Though his appearance improved as he grew older and put on some weight and dressed better, he still gave an impression of being a counter-jumper" (MacKenzie & MacKenzie, 1973, p. 112).

He remained involved in one way or another with Isabel through-out his life and gave her financial support. Even though they divorced, he never fully separated psychologically from her. Like many persons with Asperger Syndrome, he was both attracted to her and wanted to get away from her – a kind of claustro-agora position. Persons with Asperger Syndrome, although they often find close emotional relationships incredibly difficult, are also very dependent on people.

Jane gave birth to two sons: George Philip (Gip) in 1901, and Frank in 1903. Soon after the birth of Gip, H. G. set off on an extended trip around southern England. He was later to write that a compromise with Jane developed: the *modus vivendi* they contrived was sound enough to hold them together to the end, but it was by no means a perfect arrangement (MacKenzie & MacKenzie, 1973). Jane suppressed any jealous impulse and gave him whatever freedom he desired. MacKenzie and MacKenzie (1973) wrote,

> There can be no doubt of Jane's rather desperate attachment to H. G. It is clear from the remaining years of their marriage that he had a continuing dependence upon her unwavering support. But it is also clear that she was willing at all costs to conciliate him, even at the price of self-abnegation. There is a hint of fear, of a desire to appease his irritability as an apprehensive parent mollifies a self-indulgent child. It is as if, in mothering little Gip, she was discovering that she had to mother her husband as well. (p. 157)

Wells was an immature personality: He was sadistic towards his wife, who showed evidence of complimentary masochism and self-effacement. Since she made no emotional demands for herself, and had no intention of divorcing him, she was left with no alternative but to accept his mistresses. This kind of relationship is not uncommon in the "Asperger marriage." It seems that H. G. could only indulge his fantasies of freedom outside marriage, and needed to retain the formal tie of marriage as an assurance of order and continuity (MacKenzie & MacKenzie, 1973).

Regarding Wells's book *Anticipations of the Reaction of Mechanical and Scientific Progress Upon Human Life and Thought*, the novelist Joseph Conrad wrote to him in 1901,

> It seems to presuppose ... a sort of select circle to which you address yourself, leaving the rest of the world outside the pale. It seems as if they had to *come in* into a rigid system, whereas I submit that Wells should *go forth*, not dropping fishing lines for particular trout but casting a wide and generous net, where there would be room for everybody ... Generally the fault I find with you is that you do not take sufficient account of human imbecility which is cunning and perfidious. (p. 167).

According to MacKenzie and MacKenzie (1973), "Conrad had hit on the very point on which Wells was most vulnerable: his inability to see why rational men should not immediately accept his reasonably self-evident convictions – and his irritable, even contemptuous dismissal of the irrational in human nature" (p. 167). This is due to his Asperger Syndrome.

Wells was combative, impatient, over-sensitive, intemperate, and given to vendettas. Within the Fabian Society, George Bernard Shaw tried to coach him in politics – how to work in a committee, how to run meetings and conduct propaganda. Like Eamon de Valera, an Irish politician who also had Asperger Syndrome (Fitzgerald, 2004), there were ambiguities in Wells's political tracts, which were to his advantage. Regarding the Fabian Society machinations, Beatrice Webb wrote that Wells's "accusations were so preposterous – his innuendos so unsavory and his little fibs so transparent that even his own followers refused to support him … he has no manners in the broadest meaning of the word" (MacKenzie & MacKenzie, 1973, p. 219). This is indicative of his Asperger Syndrome. Shaw wrote to him: "You are forgetting your committee manners, if a man can be said to forget what he never knew." Even Leslie Haden Guest, a militant supporter of Wells within the Fabians, wrote to him, "You will make it easier by endeavoring to imagine the possibility that your views & judgments may occasionally be wrong. My fear is that your mental peculiarities may – despite the great value of your ideas & your writings – isolate you in the socialist movement & render any attempt to realize your ideas very difficult" (MacKenzie & MacKenzie, 1973, p. 220).

Shaw felt that Wells had all the sins he ascribed to his colleagues – touchiness, dogmatism, irresponsibility; to these must be added "every other petulance of which a spoilt child" is capable. Multiply these to the millionth power "and you will still fall short of the truth about Wells. Yet the worse he behaved the more he was indulged, and the more he was indulged the worse he behaved" (MacKenzie & MacKenzie, 1973, p. 220). He used projection and was paranoid about people in a general sense. The Fabian executive committee commented on his "incurable delusion … that the executive committee is a conspiracy of rogues to thwart and annoy him." Persons with Asperger Syndrome often have paranoid ideas. He clearly was tactless, wanted to have his own way, wanted to control everything – all suggestive of Asperger Syndrome. Wells was also novelty seeking or sensation seeking – a rather hyperactive, exhausting host, interested in inventing new games or improving old ones, and highly impetuous. The writer Frank Swinnerton described weekends at H. G. and Jane's house as 'whirls of unceasing activity" and H. G. as "the animated, unexhausted, inexhaustible talker" (MacKenzie & MacKenzie, 1973, p. 307). Persons with Asperger Syndrome often have hyperkinetic syndrome also.

"When he felt frustrated, H. G. was liable to pick petty quarrels with his critics, and in the spring of 1932 he had such an exchange with Leonard Woolf, who had unwisely quoted a quip from an unnamed Oxford don to the effect that Wells was a 'thinker who cannot think'" (MacKenzie & MacKenzie, 1973, p. 371). Persons with Asperger Syndrome do have problems with thinking – they think in a particular way. According to MacKenzie and MacKenzie (1973),

> As the years passed … he came to thrive on frustration as if he could experience the world only when he was in conflict with it … The heroes of his early novels were little men crushed by life. After Wells had proved to himself that success was possible, his spokesmen became more masterful characters whose aim was to bring order to a world full of waste and chaos and whose lives followed a similar trajectory

to his own. Yet they remained driven creatures, as
restless as their author, equally at odds with a social
system that brought them material rewards but eventually disillusioned and destroyed them. (p. 239)

Wells's novel *Tono-Bunjay* had strong elements of autobiography,
but he was furious when this was pointed out, and threatened
to "trace the *Fool* who started this to his lair and cut his obscene
throat." He also reacted furiously to Beatrice Webb's mild criticism
of the book. Wells often thought there were conspiracies against
him, although he was more the cause than the victim of troubles
within the Fabian Society. MacKenzie and MacKenzie (1973)
pointed out, "During his Fabian phase ... he transferred his atten-
tions to impressionable young people who were more vulnerable
and more likely to become emotionally entangled with him, and
he increasingly sought refuge in their flattery from the humiliating
defeats he received at the hands of their elders" (p. 246).

Unconsciously he was always looking for a woman who would cure
the problems that arose from his Asperger Syndrome. This would
be the ideal woman. He engaged in frequent and blatant infidelities. His second marriage became a prison like the first – as Mac-
Kenzie and MacKenzie observed, though he always related to her
as "Jane," he was aware that there was a secret "Catherine" whom
he had failed to reach.

He was tactless about his novelty-seeking relationships with other
women. Jane was able to hide the upsets that she felt because of his
behavior. As the perfect Asperger wife, she patiently picked up the

loose ends that trailed behind him as he bustled through life, and catered for the stream of visitors that H. G. needed to stimulate him when he was at home and wanted distraction from his writing (MacKenzie & MacKenzie, 1973).

He shrugged off on Jane all the petty inconveniences of household and domestic affairs that tried his patience – persons with Asperger Syndrome strongly dislike housework. Jane suffered greatly from loneliness and longing. Swinnerton described her as follows: "an amusing mixture of terror and confidence ... Her voice was small and insignificant; she had no manner; and her conversation was merely that of one who – sometimes desperately – introduced topics for others to embroider ... She never seemed quite free from painful concern lest some hitch, some argument, some breakdown in conviviality should occur ... She would look anxious, almost frightened" (MacKenzie & MacKenzie, 1973, p. 261). Beatrice Webb wrote that Jane had an ugly absence of spontaneity of thought and feeling. She was a masochistic housewife, accepting Wells keeping photographs of his women friends in his room and meeting them socially.

Jane appears also to have had some of Wells's traits. According to MacKenzie and MacKenzie, the evidence suggests that the tragedy of their estrangement lay less in the differences that he stressed than in the likenesses he overlooked. Asperger husbands tend, unconsciously, to seek out Asperger wives. After Jane's death Wells wrote, "She stuck to me so sturdily that in the end I stuck to myself." MacKenzie and MacKenzie (1973) noted, "Wells, who always expected too much from people and felt betrayed when they disappointed him, was never 'let down' by Jane. She accepted as much of his life as he was willing to give her, and acquiesced in the fact that the rest of it – including his passions – lay outside the scope of their marriage. She was thus able to tolerate a situation that most women would have found intolerable" (p. 263). This reminds one of W. B. Yeats' wife, who helped him find mistresses (Fitzgerald, 2004). Indeed, when one of Wells's mistresses, Amber Reeves, was pregnant, Jane "did the practical thing and went out and bought the baby clothes" (p. 264).

The Irish writer Rebecca West, with whom Wells had a long relationship and a son, wrote,

> He would go away after a happy time and have to stay away and I would get furious letters alluding to imaginary misfortunes and failures on my part, and this would go on for ten days or so, to my great distress, and then he would come back and there would be complete pleasantness. Or there would be some trouble with the servants and he would then tell me that I was causing all such difficulties by my incompetence and would accuse me of dwelling on these difficulties, if not actually causing them in order that he should leave Jane and marry me. (MacKenzie & MacKenzie, 1973, p. 340)

He was using an enormous amount of projection here, and paranoid behavior is typical of Asperger Syndrome. Rebecca also wrote, "If Jane divorced him and I married H. G. we would have had a ghastly life. H. G.'s sense of guilt would have thrown him off balance" (p. 340). This was his severe autistic superego. Rebecca had a "half-life" with H. G. A half-life is generally all that a person with Asperger Syndrome can offer a partner, if even that.

Rebecca also said, "He went round and round like a rat in a maze" in the last year of their relationship (MacKenzie & MacKenzie, 1973, p. 338). This is both hyperkinetic and autistic. He did not create this claustrophobic world – it was part of his Asperger Syndrome. Gradually Rebecca "grew less tolerant of H. G.'s shortcomings – his selfishness, his vanity, his disregard of her work. 'He never read more than a page or two of any of my books,' she recalled." This was probably because of his autism. She described him as "enormously vain, irascible, and in a fantasy world" (MacKenzie & MacKenzie, 1973, p. 339).

Narrow Interests/Obsessiveness

Wells was fascinated as a young man by "compact encyclopedias, which summarized philosophical doctrines, scientific ideas and historical events." He engaged in much solitary study, having "an insatiable desire for knowledge and a talent for self-expression" (MacKenzie & MacKenzie, 1973, p. 41). These are Asperger traits.

When Wells was writing *The Island of Dr. Moreau*, "he touched the spring of creative energy which enabled him to produce new work in a flood ... He wrote almost as though he were in a trance, detaching himself from money troubles and shutting out the uneasy distraction of his domestic situation. He was in a state of repressed anger," having just split up with Isabel (MacKenzie & MacKenzie, 1973, p. 107).

He was obsessed with the salvation of humankind – probably as a surrogate for the repair of his personal Asperger Syndrome. He was always fascinated by science and scientific developments: This is common in persons with Asperger Syndrome.

Routines/Control

At the age of 14, as a draper's apprentice, Wells used the imagery of imprisonment to describe his plight. The idea of imprisonment, or being locked in, is characteristic of a sense that many persons with Asperger Syndrome experience, particularly when they are not doing what they want. Wells would later apply it to his marriages. Control was very important to him – he said that in the drapery, "The unendurable thing about it was that I was never master of my own attention" (MacKenzie & MacKenzie, 1973, p. 41). When he had to become an Anglican communicant in order to get a teaching job, he felt a deep shame at this betrayal of his conscience, because it undermined "the queer little mood of obduracy" which he felt to be vital to his sense of identity (MacKenzie & MacKenzie, 1973, p. 48).

Wells was a workaholic, extremely driven, and also very driving in his determination to get others to do his wishes. He was over-controlling with his publishers and at social gatherings, which he tended to dominate. Beatrice Webb quoted him as saying, "I don't believe in tolerance, you have got to fight against anything being taught anybody which seems to you harmful, you have got to struggle to get your own creed taught" (MacKenzie & MacKenzie, 1973, p. 191). She felt that his conceit was positively disabling, and that he was in a state of unstable equilibrium. Many years later Wells admitted that he had shown bad judgment and vanity in his dealings with the Fabian Society, yet he insisted that his motives had been misunderstood and that he had been fundamentally right.

According to MacKenzie and MacKenzie (1973), Wells "felt more and more compelled to talk at his readers through his characters, rather than to allow them the room they needed to emerge as personalities" (p. 193). This was a flaw in his work that other notable writers discerned from time to time. People with Asperger Syndrome often present as prophets. In 1906, Wells found it galling that praise for his talents as a prophet and propagandist was not to be translated immediately and uncritically into acceptance of his grandiose plans for transforming the Fabian Society (MacKenzie & MacKenzie, 1973). He was more interested in fantasies of omnipotence than in detailed work and painstaking organization.

In Wells's 1920 book *The Secret Places of the Heart*, the main character, Richmond Hardy, "turns to the psychiatrist Dr. Martineau for help because his life has become meaningless. This novel reveals that by the end of 1920, and despite his recent success and increasing wealth and prestige, H. G. was in a desperate state of mind – as restless and uncertain of himself as he had been during earlier crises in his career" (MacKenzie & MacKenzie, 1973, p. 330). Existential questions and the meaning of life are always critical for persons with Asperger Syndrome (see for example *The Meaning of Life* by A. J. Ayer – Ayer had Asperger Syndrome; Fitzgerald, 2005).

Odette Keun, who had a long sexual relationship with Wells, became bitterly disillusioned. In 1934, reviewing his autobiography, she wrote that she had begun as a disciple of this "gigantic personality" who "imposed his dream on all of us," and she now attempted to define the flaw in his genius. This "noisy, rude, selfish, sulky, ungrateful, vulgar, and entirely insuppressible" little boy had been miraculously "over-sensitized." H. G. had no moral discipline, Huxley's rationalism had destroyed his religious sense, and his behavior depended wholly upon the impulsive likes and dislikes of an "outraged ego." He had no humility, and for him life was a game rather than a vocation. Though he won an enormous following, he was a player rather than a true leader, and he would never take responsibility for the role in which he had cast himself. His "unparalleled capacity for shifting and changing" was "shattering for the men and women who aspired to be disciples." (MacKenzie & MacKenzie, 1973, pp. 385–386)

The writer Ford Madox Ford found that in conversation Wells "monologued in a conversational tone until he had led the discussion into the strategic position he had chosen – and then defended it … He let his hearers say a word or two and then suppressed them either with superior knowledge or a quip that changed the course of discussion" (MacKenzie & MacKenzie, 1973, p. 143). This is typical Asperger control of conversation.

Wells described his routine to Charlie Chaplin: "When you have written your pages in the morning, attended your correspondence in the evening, and have nothing further to do, then comes that hour when you are bored; that is the time for sex" (MacKenzie & MacKenzie, 1973, p. 388).

Language/Humor

H. G. "was never a good speaker. He described himself at Fabian meetings as 'speaking haltingly on the verge of the inaudible, addressing my tie through a cascade moustache that was no help at all, correcting myself as though I were a manuscript under treatment'" (MacKenzie & MacKenzie, 1973, p. 185). This has the hallmarks of an Asperger speech and language problem. MacKenzie and MacKenzie noted that Wells lacked a real sense of humor behind the seductive charm, the bubbling fun, the vulgar larks and Cockney capers.

Lack of Empathy

Joseph Conrad, though he admired much of Wells's writing, wrote to him, "The difference between us is fundamental. You don't care for humanity but think they are to be improved. I love humanity but know they are not" (Hart-Davis, 1952, p. 168).

Wells was interested in utopias but distrusted the masses. He applauded Malthus as well as Darwin and was interested in eugenics, having decided that "the best insurance against the kind of evolutionary regression which haunted his earlier writing is to secure the survival of the fittest by the elimination of the unfit." He felt if the "unfit" were protected, society would be "swamped in their fecundity," and also that the "unfit" can exist only on sufferance, and that the "New Republicans" would not "hesitate to kill when that sufferance is abused" (MacKenzie & MacKenzie, 1973, p. 166). Wells advocated birth control and even sterilization to counter the masses' propensity to breed useless, troublesome, and miserable children – clearly there are parallels with Nazism here.

MacKenzie and MacKenzie (1973) wrote of Wells's lack of any stable frame for his attitudes and conduct, and a carelessness for his effect on his wives, his mistresses, his publishers, political associates and friends. This made him unable to distinguish between small and great annoyances and between trivial notions and sweeping principles, or to scale his responses to the relative importance of what was said or done to him. Wells was an ideologist and an outsider.

In trying to take over the Fabian Society he went "too far, too fast, and [was] rude to everyone as well" (MacKenzie & MacKenzie, 1973, p. 199). This shows his tactlessness. It was not unusual for him to alienate his supporters because of his lack of empathy – in the Fabian Society he forced a choice between him and Beatrice and Sidney Webb and failed to get a single vote in a meeting full of his sympathizers – an astonishing feat, according to MacKenzie and MacKenzie, and one that he was later to repeat. Shaw considered him "too reckless of etiquette," and advised him, "Generally speaking, you must identify yourself frankly with us, and not play the critical outsider and the satirist … there are limits to our powers of enduring humiliations that are totally undeserved" (MacKenzie & MacKenzie, 1973, p. 200). Shaw also told him, "You must study people's corns when you go clog dancing."

As we have seen, Wells tended to be away from home a lot, but Jane concealed her depression and loneliness. He was an Asperger husband and totally insensitive to her. She took his insensitivity and absorbed it. She once wrote to him: "If I set out to make a comfortable home for you & do work in [*sic*], I merely succeed in contriving a place where you are bored to death" (MacKenzie & MacKenzie, 1973, p. 202).

Wells was confused about emotions and inclined to be touchy; he "always flew into a rage when anyone suggested that his books were in any way immoral. He seems to have no more insight into the implications of his books than his own behavior" (MacKenzie & MacKenzie, 1973, p. 267). This is consistent with Asperger Syndrome. Beatrice Webb further noted "his total incapacity for decent conduct ... What annoyed him was our puritan view of life and our insistence on the fulfillment of obligations ... he passed back again to ... sexual dissipation and vehemently objected to and disliked what he knew would be our judgment of it" (MacKenzie & MacKenzie, 1973, p. 270). He was tactless in the way he lampooned people and had the capacity to be very self-destructive.

In his book *The New Machiavelli*, Wells "permitted his life to sprawl into the novel so carelessly that self-indulgence had ruined it as a work of art" (MacKenzie & MacKenzie, 1973, p. 278). Persons with Asperger Syndrome have problems with boundaries. Because of their lack of empathy and problems with theory of mind, they often overstep the boundaries and get themselves into trouble. At this time Wells had determined that all his books must present his notions of reconstructing the world: This was somewhat megalomaniacal. MacKenzie and MacKenzie noted that in his later novels Wells "indulged himself in his past, relying on his power of vivid description and good story-telling to obscure the fact that he was unable to use his experience at the emotional level required to transmute life into art" (p. 280). This was a failing consistent with Asperger Syndrome.

Odette Keun wrote that Wells was flawed by his "brutality ... He turned intellectual debate into a private quarrel ... he ridiculed his adversaries. This idol of course … is cruel. He had no conviction of reality about either humanity or the individual. The game was the thing" (MacKenzie & MacKenzie, 1973, p. 386). Here Keun is describing the problems of an Asperger man. This is a typical Asperger Syndrome attitude to sex. For example, Wells told William Somerset Maugham that "the need to satisfy sexual instincts had nothing to do with love. It was a purely physiological matter." According to MacKenzie and MacKenzie (1973), "It was actually more than that: Wells found sex a vital anodyne for despair" (p. 307).

In 1935, on a visit to the United States, Wells visited William Randolph Hearst's fantastic castle at San Simeon, where he delivered a long speech after dinner, "saying in his whispering squeaky voice that the past hundred years in American history were nothing for Americans to be proud of, and that since 1920 Americans had behaved like idiots. They had the chance to rule the world, but because of greed and pusillanimity had lost all their chances. The Americans at the table looked blue and were very polite" (MacKenzie & MacKenzie, 1973, p. 393). This was a typical tactless Asperger speech, ignoring the context. Beatrice Webb concluded, "H. G. in fact expected too much from his fellow men, and that he therefore felt misunderstood, misrepresented and disappointed" (MacKenzie & MacKenzie, 1973, p. 399) – again, an Asperger position.

According to MacKenzie and MacKenzie (1973), "H. G. was cocky, tactless and rude almost without being aware of the harm he was doing himself; but it was not just manners that made him so tiresome that people found it hard to work with him even when they agreed with his ideas" (p. 459). These authors attribute his idiosyncrasies to his upbringing in a disgruntled household; we attribute them to his Asperger Syndrome. He showed a classical Asperger failure to "hold the line between the worlds of fiction and fact," which "led him to so parade his sexual career that it became unusually pertinent to his public careers" (MacKenzie & MacKenzie, 1973, p. 459). This lack of reality testing is possibly one of the reasons why Asperger Syndrome is sometimes misdiagnosed as schizophrenia.

Naivety/Childishness

Because of Wells's immature personality, he often enjoyed "boyish games," and went to elaborate lengths in organizing and playing them with his guests and others. His "boyhood imagination was still active: H. G. liked nothing better than fantasies in which his enemies were routed" (MacKenzie & MacKenzie, 1973, p. 231). Indeed, Shaw compared him to a spoilt, petulant child.

During World War I, H. G. was on an advisory committee that produced a memorandum to the Foreign Office, but he was "naïve about the realities of power politics," being unaware that Britain had made secret agreements and that "he and his colleagues were being cynically used as decoys by a government which had no intention of turning fine phrases into deeds" (MacKenzie & MacKenzie, 1973, p. 307).

Moods

Toward the end of the nineteenth century, "The frantic writing of the stories had proved therapeutically effective and enabled him to find the thread of purpose he teased out through life" (MacKenzie & MacKenzie, 1973, p. 130). Wells suffered bouts of depression and petulance and experienced temper tantrums and "days in incapable rage" (Asperger rage is common). Writing was Wells's anti-depressant and kept him alive. As a young man, frustrated with his lot as a draper's apprentice, he had contemplated suicide.

Chapter 17 in MacKenzie and MacKenzie (1973) is entitled "A Tangle of Moods and Impulses" – a phrase Wells used in describing himself, with reference to his relationship with Jane. He had a vindictive temper, and became depressed and disappointed as he grew older. Notwithstanding his behavior, Wells was an idealist – he had a very big ego ideal and an autistic superego.

Wells was capable of being an aggressive, nasty, vindictive man; he was also a very tormented man. In 1931, his book *What Are We to Do With Our Lives?* set out his current plan for the salvation of mankind and revealed his feelings of "irritation and impotence at his failure to influence the course of events" (MacKenzie & MacKenzie, 1973, p. 367). Persons with Asperger Syndrome often turn into gurus, or try to.

A cook in the Wells household aptly advised a new governess that Wells "can be pretty prickly at times, and most exasperating and impatient. It all depends on his mood. There are days when he goes skylarking about the house and garden like a schoolboy home for the holidays, and the next day everybody seems to get in his way and annoy him. So beware" (MacKenzie & MacKenzie, 1973, p. 230). This kind of moodiness is characteristic of Asperger Syndrome.

Wells often felt stress; for example, in 1897 he wrote "I have been very much worried by a commission for two short stories and an inability to get up to the mark with them – a consequent disorganization – nerves wrong – sleeplessness, swearing, weeping" (MacKenzie & MacKenzie, 1973, p. 133). He suffered from a great deal of mental distress, and indeed mental ill health, in his life. Another cause of stress was that he became embroiled in squabbles with publishers, partly due to his paranoid stance with regard to life and to people. Certainly, in close relationships he suffered from claustrophobia.

According to MacKenzie and MacKenzie (1973), "Many of the books in which Wells explored his own life concluded with a dying fall, but the obsession with death had never been so explicit as it became in the group of books written after 1921" (p. 338). Persons with Asperger Syndrome have a lot of death anxiety.

Odette Keun noted that when Wells was irritated he could be ferocious and quite demonic. She also said, "He was never sane enough to forget – much less to the throw off – his personal bitterness." For Keun, "Wells's towering self-pity and abrasive pettiness had gradually eroded the idol she had worshipped" (MacKenzie & MacKenzie, 1973, p. 372). A series of bitter rows between them led to H. G. "characteristically seeing himself as the injured party." Such self-pity is commonly shown by persons with Asperger Syndrome.

Identity Diffusion

Wells had a fragmented sense of self, or multiple selves, as persons with Asperger Syndrome often do. MacKenzie and MacKenzie (1973) noted, "There was no cohesion in his life, or in his work" (p. 335) and that he "avoided the implications of his own dualism" (p. 408). At a certain point during World War I, "He was no longer in a marriage punctuated by infidelities: he was beginning a double life, in which he switched moods as quickly as he doffed his role as husband and host at Easton and, at the other end of a train journey, appeared at Rebecca's house in the part of a lover. The magic transformations which had characterized the *doppelganger* figures in his stories had now become habitual in his own life" (MacKenzie & MacKenzie, 1973, p. 305). This is suggestive of autistic multiple selves.

Similarly, Wells wrote of his conduct during his affair with Amber Reeves, "I was, by twists and turns, two entirely different people" – a "schizoid state of mind" that MacKenzie and MacKenzie (1973, p. 451) explained by reference to his parents' contrasting and conflicting personalities but that we feel is better accounted for by Asperger Syndrome. MacKenzie and MacKenzie (1973) noted that he picked up psychological catchphrases and served them half-baked; in the postscript to his autobiography he covered them in bland Jungian sauce, and could never achieve a coherent explanation of any of the questions he asked himself. This was because of his autistic lack of a sense of self.

Political Views

As previously noted, some of Wells's political and social opinions had much in common with Nazism. In later life, his political interests were "on the eccentric fringes of the Labour Movement. He had a distinctive position in politics which could not be neatly classified in contemporary terms as 'right' or 'left,' and anyone who tried to locate him along the spectrum found puzzling contradictions" (MacKenzie & MacKenzie, 1973, p. 375). This rather diffuse stance perhaps makes more sense if viewed through the lens of his Asperger Syndrome. (After Eamon de Valera spoke, people didn't know whether he was for or against the topic of discussion.) For example, Wells admired large-scale planning and approved of the Soviet Union but simultaneously denounced Marxism as nonsense and Stalinism as a tyranny. This shows Asperger contradictions and confusion in thinking. The large-scale planning, of course, would fit with the Asperger wish for total control. After meeting Stalin, "H. G. came away feeling that he had 'never met a man more candid, fair and honest' and that it was to these qualities 'and to nothing occult and sinister' that Stalin owed his power" (MacKenzie & MacKenzie, 1973, p. 380). Here Wells was showing his massive lack of empathy and lack of judgment.

Late in life Wells wrote that the common man "finds himself menaced unaccountably and impeded and frustrated at every turn, in his will to live happily" (MacKenzie & MacKenzie, 1973, p. 432). This might be a good description of a person struggling with Asperger Syndrome.

Conclusion

On the title page of their fascinating biography of H. G. Wells, Norman and Jeanne MacKenzie include these lines from Matthew Arnold's "Empedocles on Etna:"

> 'Tis not the times, 'tis not the sophists vex him;
> There is some root of suffering in himself,
> Some secret and unfollow'd vein of woe,
> Which makes the time look black and sad to him

We think this "vein of woe" can be seen, in Wells's case, as a metaphor for Asperger Syndrome.

CHAPTER 13

John Broadus Watson
(1878–1958)

The American psychologist John Broadus Watson was born near Greenville, South Carolina, and educated at Furman University and the University of Chicago. He later became professor of psychology at Johns Hopkins University, where he developed the school of psychology known as behaviorism. This approach sought to abandon the concept of consciousness and restrict psychology to the study of behavior, with the objective of explaining, predicting, and controlling behavior. Watson made the first systematic studies of rat behavior, and had a major influence on the development of psychological research.

Due to an extramarital affair with a student, Watson was forced to leave Johns Hopkins in 1920. His subsequent career was in advertising, where he sought to apply the psychological principles he had derived. After retiring in 1945, he led a reclusive life on a small farm in Connecticut, drinking heavily. He died in 1958, at the age of 80.

According to Buckley (1989),

> More than any other psychologist of his generation, he shaped the image of the profession in the public mind. Moreover, his popularized vision of a science of behavior control stirred the imagination of a new generation of psychologists. It was a young B. F. Skinner who as a student glimpsed the "possibility of technological applications" in Watson's *Behaviorism* ... (p. 160)

Although his ideas were often contentious (e.g., on the rearing of children and the role of women in society), many psychologists regard Watson as one of the greatest psychologists of the twentieth century. This chapter presents evidence that Watson had Asperger Syndrome.

Family and Childhood

Watson was the fourth of six children of Pickens Butler Watson and Emma Roe. His father was a drinker, brawler, and former Confederate soldier; his mother, a devout Baptist, was regarded as far below her husband on the social scale, with the result that the family was ostracized.

Watson grew up first on a small farm and then in the town of Greenville. His volatile father was absent from the family home for long periods. Watson had difficulty in adjusting to town life and showed aggressive behavior.

Possible Indicators of Asperger Syndrome

Social Behavior

At Furman University, Watson described himself as unsocial and made few friends. He had an aloof, almost shy disposition and in later life became a virtual recluse. One professor remembered him as "bright" but "more interested in ideas and theories than … people" (Buckley, 1989, p. 11). According to Buckley (1989), his constant striving for achievement and approval was often sabotaged by "acts of sheer obstinacy and impulsiveness" (p. 12).

Not surprisingly, Watson wanted "a place where daily living can be taught" – daily living was clearly what he had difficulty with. After graduating from Furman, he had a brief spell as principal of Batesburg Institute, a small private academy; one of his students later recalled that Watson "kept to himself and avoided the social life of the community" (Buckley, 1989, pp. 13–14).

At the University of Chicago, where he continued his studies, Watson was "an ambitious, extremely status-conscious young man, anxious to make his mark upon the world but wholly unsettled as to his choice of profession and desperately insecure about his lack of means and social sophistication" (Buckley, 1989, p. 39). Like many psychologists even today, he longed for the prestige of an MD degree.

Watson had major interpersonal difficulties at the university. According to Buckley (1989), "When Watson submitted a request for additional laboratory equipment, some ill-considered remarks contained in the request were taken by William Rainey Harper (president of the University of Chicago) to be either an 'indication of insanity, or intentional impertinence'" (p. 51). As a psychologist in World War I, he again had major interpersonal difficulties, describing the experience as a nightmare. His racism and social insecurity were evident: "Talk of putting a Negro in uniform! It is nothing [in comparison] to making a Major or Lieutenant Colonel of most of the Rotary Club men who went in as officers in the American Army (West Point and Naval Academy men excluded)" (Buckley, 1989, p. 106). Harold Ickes, his brother-in-law, claimed that Watson was not liked or respected at the university.

"Laboratory experiments that involved human participants made Watson uncomfortable, and he always acted unnaturally under those conditions, which he described as stuffy and artificial" (Buckley,

1989, p. 40). He turned with relief to the study of animals. After his retirement, his favorite companions were the animals on his farm. It is common for persons with autism to prefer animals to people.

Notwithstanding Watson's professional concerns with order, his personal life was "tempestuous and sometimes chaotic" – he chose women who were "young, impressionable and, initially at least, awed by him," and married one of his students, Mary Ickes, in 1904 (Buckley, 1989, p. 50). Watson was often a willing mentor to his female students, but he was extremely uncomfortable with women as professional peers. The marriage was disastrous for both parties, and ended sensationally after 16 years.

The cause of the divorce, and of Watson's dismissal from Johns Hopkins University, was his affair with Rosalie Rayner, a graduate student who was his research assistant. According to Buckley (1989), Watson was convinced that his professional stature would render him impervious to any censure of his private life, and he completely misjudged the sensibilities of the authorities at Johns Hopkins. His chances of securing another academic position were ruined by the massive nationwide publicity that attended his divorce hearing.

Narrow Interests/Obsessiveness

Watson was a very insecure man. He worked extremely hard, very long hours, and was hugely ambitious. Buckley (1989) noted that his obsession with achievement reflected deep anxieties about failure and success, and his driving ambition precluded any compromise with competing ideas. Extreme narrowness and inability to listen to anyone else were typical of him.

Watson became convinced of the notion that a human being is simply a biological mechanism, and produced a theory of emotions whose development depended entirely on external conditioning. He viewed the self as defined by the choice of one's career. Adolf Meyer, the great U.S. psychiatrist, made a wide-ranging attack on Watson's views and methods. He complained bitterly to Watson about the rigidity of his position: "You would like to see all the psycho-pathological facts treated under the paradigma of conditioned reflexes, with the elimination of *all* and every reference to psyche or mental, etc." (Buckley, 1989, p. 90). Buckley goes on to state, "Meyer thought Watson's attitude to be 'immature' and '*hopelessly narrow*' … [he] thought Watson's position to be 'psychophobic' and suggested Watson's rigidity implied something deeper than a disagreement on principle." In addition, "Meyer was particularly annoyed with Watson's use of obfuscating terminology that masked what he considered to be a crude positivism that placed severe limits on the possibility of understanding the complexities of human experience" (p. 91).

Meyer also accused Watson of shutting out everything that might confuse his outlook and thought that Watson needed "a broader human outlook and balance of judgment if he is not to be as much of a danger to the development of psychology as he is a real boon" (Buckley, 1989, p. 117). Watson was completely single-minded: There is little doubt that he was the ultimate mechanical man, who promoted a connection between the development of psychology as a science and its use as a technology. In his promotion of behaviorism he tended, like many persons with high-functioning autism, to be propagandist and evangelistic.

He read huge numbers of western novels and detective stories, just like Ludwig Wittgenstein, who is also thought to have had Asperger Syndrome (Fitzgerald, 2004).

Routines/Control

Watson saw the goal of behaviorism as the gathering of facts necessary to enable it to predict and to control human behavior. He was extraordinarily authoritarian and controlling. According to Buckley (1989), "Watson's preoccupation with the control of emotions reflected his lifelong struggle with strong feelings that constantly threatened to overturn his carefully maintained equilibrium" (p. 120), and "Since Watson claimed to have refuted the idea of the inner world of the self once and for all, behaviorism became ... an instrumental rationality for manipulating the control of emotions" (p. 121). Buckley (1989) pointed out, "William Butler Yeats was not alone among Watson's contemporaries in seeing the world as a place where 'things fall apart.' As an antidote, behaviorism was unambiguous, straightforward, and seemed to offer a hope of certainty for those who so desperately sought it" (p. 123). (Yeats also had high-functioning autism [Fitzgerald, 2004].)

Some aspects of Watson's preoccupation with control can be seen as sinister: He saw behaviorism as providing the tools with which psychologists would become social engineers. Criminals and social deviants who failed to respond to reconditioning should be "restrained always and made to earn their daily bread in vast manufacturing and agricultural institutions, escape from which is impossible" (Buckley, 1989, p. 146). How psychologists could follow such a man is hard to understand.

Watson said that the measures he envisaged implied the elimination of legal process: He looked forward to the day when "all law books are burned in some great upheaval of nature" and "all lawyers and jurists ... decide to become behaviorists" (Buckley, 1989, p. 165). At such a time, that enforcement would hardly be necessary because his utopian citizens would be conditioned from birth to function in a manner predetermined by a hierarchy of technocrats (Buckley, 1989).

Child-rearing and education were fundamental to Watson's vision: "The success or failure of such a society depended upon the absolute control of an educational process that would function, not as a means of acquiring knowledge, but as the instrument of the individual's socialization" (Buckley, 1989, p. 166). Watson made outrageous statements about thumb sucking, warning that it bred "introversion, dependent individuals, and possibly confirmed masturbators" (Buckley, 1989, p. 152). The uncontrollable child was a result of bad handling through a series of "negative conditioned reflexes." (As well as being largely untrue, this is extremely simplistic.)

Watson conditioned a 9-month-old infant – Albert B. – to fear animals. It is interesting from the ethical point of view that he made no attempt to recondition Albert afterwards. He even suggested that children could be conditioned by means of a system of electric shocks to avoid objects that they were not allowed to touch.

Watson was uncomfortable with women as professional peers – he could relate only to younger people and was attracted to women who were sufficiently young and inexperienced to be easily controlled. In later life he was obsessed with the pursuit of women.

Not surprisingly, behaviorism had its critics. According to Buckley,

> This notion of control in behaviorism disturbed
> Bertrand Russell. Although he supported Watson in
> his efforts to demystify the thinking process, Russell
> saw potential for abuse by a technocratic elite. Ex-
> ploitation of behavioristic techniques of control, he
> warned, could result in a society wherein the official
> class of "thinkers" dominated a passive class of "feel-
> ers." (1989, p. 119)

The psychologist Edward Bradford Titchener stated that "The practical goal of the control of behavior" gave behaviorism "the stamp of technology": In Titchener's opinion, Watson's wish "to exchange a science for a technology" was out of the question (Buckley, 1989, p. 80).

Watson defined behavior as a biological problem while ignoring consciousness, insisting that psychology was a purely objective experimental branch of natural science, with its theoretical goal being nothing less than the prediction and control of behavior. By implication, Watson was clear about what, in his opinion, psychology was *not*. It was not a stepchild of philosophy. Speculations about the nature of the mind that could not be tested in the laboratory had no place in an experimental branch of natural science. He wanted psychology to be independent of philosophy.

Also, according to Buckley (1989), "Watson's preoccupation with being busy suggests something other than a search for pleasure; his constant mechanical motion more resembles a flight into the *oblivion* of activity" (p. 178). Buckley noted that Watson "steadfast-ly refused to reflect upon his own life. His scant autobiographical writings are curiously flat and omit much more than they reveal" (p. 179). (They are therefore like the writings of the philosophers A. J. Ayer and William Quine.) It was due to his high-function-ing autism that he had problems with autobiography. According to Buckley (1989), he had a "rigid, one-dimensional view of life that could tolerate no ambiguity. What many took to be callousness or indifference was, in reality, an extreme sensitivity to the uncertain-ties of daily existence" (p. 179).

Watson's youngest son later remarked that growing up with his fa-ther was like a business proposition. Their relationship was "devoid of emotional interchange" (Buckley, 1989, p. 180), but the children were expected to be extremely meticulous in their bodily habits and punctual at meals and at bedtime.

Language/Humor
Watson "minimized the importance of language as a factor distin-guishing human beings from animals. Language, he believed, was merely a more elaborate and complex category of behavior" (Buck-ley, 1989, p. 54). Some of his ideas were extraordinarily similar to those of Wittgenstein.

Watson's own use of language does not appear to have been problem-atic. He does not seem to have shown a developed sense of humor.

Lack of Empathy
Watson felt that "the psychologist should not be unduly concerned

with the individual patient's interests when conducting experiments" (Buckley, 1989, p. 94). This appears to be an unempathetic and unethical attitude. He was also extremely unempathetic with those around him. At the University of Chicago he was notorious for his lack of tact.

Buckley (1989) noted that "Watson was not bothered 'in the least' by hearing his children cry … his temperament as a father was hardly warm. His daughter recalled that the only time her father was physically affectionate towards her was when he departed for Europe during World War I – and then he merely kissed her on the forehead" (p. 55).

According to Buckley (1989), Robert M. Yerkes thought that Watson, at times, resorted to unnecessary criticism calculated to provoke antagonism. Herbert Spencer Jennings considered Watson's position to be strangely wooden and narrow.

Watson was a misogynist, who believed that a life in the business world made women unfit for marriage, and characterized women who dared to challenge the restrictions of such traditional social roles as maladjusted. His vision of behavioral training for women entailed study of the use of cosmetics, how to stay thin, how to be successful hostesses, and to put on the intellectual attainments that go into the making of a beautiful, graceful, wise woman. As Buckley (1989) pointed out, "all of the wives and mothers in Watson's utopia were beautiful and graceful because, as he chillingly put it, 'large women and the occasional ill-favored woman are not allowed to breed'" (p. 164). Buckley observed that the function of the "biologically unfit" in Watson's world is unclear.

Watson believed that most mothers begin to destroy their children the moment they are born, and advised parents to treat their children as if they were young adults. Buckley (1989) correctly described the following advice as perhaps his most notorious: "Never hug and kiss them, never let them sit on your lap" (p. 162). This sounds like a recipe for autistic-style parenting. Watson did not believe that affection would efficiently serve societal needs, and even argued that affection could potentially subvert the social order.

Watson didn't shirk from applying his principles to his own children. In his book *Behaviorism*, he described how "he subjected his eldest son, Billy (then about three years old), to an experiment to determine his instinct for jealousy by appearing to physically abuse his wife in front of the child. Terrified and confused, Billy "cried, kicked and tugged at his father's leg and struck with his hand. Yet Watson continued the display of violence until "the youngster was genuinely disturbed and the experiment had to be discontinued" (Buckley, 1989, p. 180). Billy committed suicide in the early 1960s.

Buckley (1989) also noted that Watson had long dreamed of an "experimental 'baby farm' where hundreds of infants of diverse racial backgrounds would be the subjects of observation and research. In his ideal world, child rearing would be brought as much as possible under laboratory control. Mothers would not know the identity of their children. Breast feeding would be prohibited, and the children would be rotated among families at four-week intervals until the age of twenty" (p. 163). This proposal is extremely bizarre and echoes the orphanages that the Nazis set up during World War II.

In Watson's utopia, there would be no mercy: When conditioning failed to cure what Watson termed the "hopelessly insane" or incurably diseased, the physician would not hesitate to put them to death (Buckley, 1989). This sounds much like what happened in fascist countries during World War II.

Naivety/Childishness

William I. Thomas, a friend who took in Watson after his divorce, stated that he was childish. Thomas observed that Watson's fault was that

> he expects instant appreciation and help from all who are allied with him and has no consciousness at all of reciprocity. He is like a child who expects petting and indulgence, but has no return … He thinks people have and must have a perpetual good opinion of him without regard to his behavior … He has scales on his eyes, and becomes quickly a pest or a comedy to all men who know him intimately … He is a good case to watch with reference to our question whether there is any age at which habits cannot be changed. (Buckley, 1989, p. 131)

Clearly, what Thomas was describing here was autistic behavior. Watson didn't understand conventional behavior, and had many immature and utopian ideas.

Motor Skills

Watson does not appear to have shown an obvious deficit in this area.

Comorbidity

Watson was a workaholic, who suffered what he called a "break-down" early in his career: "Weeks of insomnia followed by a period of enforced rest during which he could sleep only in a well-lighted place were the manifestations of what he later described as 'a typical *angst*'" (Buckley, 1989, p. 44). He also showed evidence of a narcissistic pathology.

Conclusion

Like Charles Darwin, Stonewall Jackson, and Nikola Tesla, John Broadus Watson appears to have met the criteria for a diagnosis of Asperger's disorder, which is defined more widely than Asperger Syndrome (i.e. neither abnormalities of speech and language nor motor clumsiness are necessary for Asperger's disorder under the American Psychiatric Association [1994] classification).

CHAPTER 14

Albert Einstein
(1879–1955)

Albert Einstein is recognized as the greatest physicist of the 20th century and ranks with Isaac Newton as one of the pre-eminent scientific figures in history. His biographer, Albrecht Fölsing (1997), wrote that no one else has ever enriched a science as Einstein enriched physics during the two decades between 1905 and 1925. Fölsing (1997) described him as "a seeker after truth, whose like we shall not see again" (p. xiii). He is best known for his theories of special and general relativity (1905 and 1916, respectively) and for elucidating the particle theory of light, but he also wrote widely on nonscientific subjects and supported various social and political causes. In 1922 he was awarded the Nobel Prize for physics; he subsequently became a major international celebrity, attracting huge media attention wherever he went.

As a young man, Einstein worked in the Swiss patent office in Berne. He married Mileva Marič in 1903. The previous year she had given birth to their daughter, who seems to have been given up for adoption. They later had two sons, born in 1904 and 1910. They separated in 1914 and divorced in 1919. Later that year Einstein married his cousin, Elsa Löwenthal (née Einstein), also divorced, who had two daughters.

Einstein served as a professor of physics at Zurich and Prague universities, and for almost 20 years was director of the Kaiser Wilhelm Physical Institute in Berlin. He left Germany for the United States after the Nazis came to power, working at Princeton University and becoming a U.S. citizen in 1940. A vehement opponent of Nazism, he warned Franklin D. Roosevelt that Germany would try to create an atomic bomb and later campaigned for control of nuclear weapons. He was offered the presidency of Israel in 1952, but declined. He died in Princeton on April 18, 1955.

Family and Childhood

Einstein was born on March 14, 1879, into a Jewish family in Ulm, a town in southern Germany whose motto was *Ulmenses sunt mathematici* (the people of Ulm are mathematicians). His parents were Pauline (née Koch) and Hermann Einstein. Pauline, 11 years younger than Hermann, was 21 years old at the time of Albert's birth. She was immediately "alarmed at the sight of his exceptionally large angular occiput and at first thought he was a monster" (Fölsing, 1997, p. 3). A large head circumference is seen in some persons with autism (Bailey, 1993).

Einstein's parents were well educated; Pauline played the piano. She was extremely stubborn and obstinate. Hermann Einstein was hardworking, "a kind and friendly man, esteemed and loved by all of his family and friends, especially those of the female sex" (Fölsing, 1997, p. 10). Neither parent attended the synagogue or practiced Jewish rites and customs. It has been suggested that Albert got his mathematical gifts from his father and his love of music from his mother, but he himself disagreed, stating that curiosity, obsession, and sheer perseverance brought him to his ideas. He seems to have been a quiet baby, and at the age of 2 was described as sweet and good. The family moved to Munich when he was 1 year old.

Although interested in all kinds of puzzles and in "making elaborate structures with building blocks and constructing houses of cards of breathtaking height" (Fölsing, 1997, p. 11), Albert was averse to play and social behavior appropriate to his age; other children regarded him as a bore. When he occasionally did take part in play, he "deliberately sought the job of umpire, which, because of his instinctive sense of justice, was gladly assigned to him" (Fölsing, 1997, p. 12). However, he had a violent temper as a young child. On one occasion, according to his sister Maja, he struck a female tutor with a chair; she "ran away in fear and was never seen again" (Fölsing, 1997, p. 12).

At school he suffered from anti-Semitism and was bullied. He had a sense of being an outsider and never stepped out of his characteristic isolation, rarely playing with other children. He had a reserved manner and an ingrained dislike of physical training and games. He never got tired when "engrossed with his beloved metal construction set, or with involved fretsaw work, or with manipulating a small hissing steam engine," but behind his "facade of adjustment," he exhibited a "dreamerlike, skeptical distancing from other people and things" (Fölsing, 1997, p. 17). He never wanted to become a soldier or to play with toy soldiers; in fact, he showed a strong antipathy to all aspects of militarism.

As an older child he associated the atmosphere of school with that of the barrack-square – in his eyes, this was the negation of everything human. His memory for words was poor, and he resented the dull, mechanized method of teaching to which he was subjected, preferring to endure punishments rather than to learn by rote. A teacher of Greek told him that he would never amount to anything.

Reflecting later on how and why he had discovered relativity theory, Einstein pointed to his slow development as a child, whereby he began to reflect on space and time only when he was grown up, whereas for an average person "anything that needs reflection on this matter he believes he did in his early childhood" (Fölsing, 1997, p. 13).

Possible Indicators of Asperger Syndrome

Social Behavior

As just noted, the young Einstein had major problems in playing with and relating to other children. He also showed evidence of temper tantrums as a child, but they receded from the age of 7 onward. The anti-Semitism he experienced as a child enhanced his sense of being an outsider. On leaving Berlin for the United States in 1931, he described himself as a migrating bird.

At Zurich Polytechnic, Einstein formed a relationship with Mileva Marić, a fellow student three years older than him. He wrote to her, "We understand one another's dark souls." After marrying Mileva, Einstein recognized that his talent for married life was somewhat limited, however. He found the duties of marriage too much. His son, Hans Albert, later attributed his parents' estrangement to the fact that his father believed that the family would take up too much of his time; he felt he had a duty to concentrate solely on his work (Fölsing, 1997). It is clear that physics gave him far more happiness than family relationships. In the mid-1920s, he fell violently in love with his secretary, Betty Neumann, but ended the relationship by writing to her that he must seek in the stars that which was denied him on earth. It is not surprising that his sons turned against him. He noted in 1915 that 11-year-old Hans Albert "wrote me a very brusque card, resolutely rejecting a tour with me" (Fölsing, 1997, p. 364).

Einstein had many relationships with women, but he "clearly intended these women, like his daughter, Lieserl, to vanish in the shadows of history," wrote Fölsing (1997, p. 617). He was not interested in connecting with individuals or human communities, describing himself as a real "loner, who never belonged wholeheartedly to the state, the homeland, my circle of friends, or even my own family, but experienced with regard to all these ties a never abating feeling of outsiderness and a need for solitude ... One experiences clearly, but without regret, the limit of communication and consonance with other people" (Fölsing, 1997, p. 620). He described his life in Berlin as that of "a Gypsy ... an unattached person, who was fond of looking at the comical side of everything" (Fölsing, 1997, p. 620).

He saw himself as a stranger everywhere. When he moved to Princeton his sense of isolation and alienation, if anything, increased; he noted, "I am not really becoming part of the human world here, for that I was too old when I arrived, and in point of fact it was no different in Berlin or in Switzerland. One is born a loner" (Fölsing, 1997, p. 688). He felt fortunate living in Princeton, largely because the Princetonians respected his need for solitude.

Although he was a pacifist, some of Einstein's writings are somewhat disturbing, showing an unsympathetic attitude to human beings; for example, "I would have no objection to the killing of worthless or even harmful individuals, I am against it only because I do not trust people, i.e., the courts. I appreciate more the quality than the quantity of human life" (Fölsing, 1997, p. 621). After World War II he "rejected humanitarian programs to help Germans suffering hardships in their destroyed country" (Fölsing, 1997, p. 727). According to Fölsing (1997), he felt happier as a lone fighter than in the atmosphere of a committee where compromise was inevitable.

Einstein remarked in 1936 that he was "living in the kind of solitude that is painful in one's youth but in one's more mature years is delicious" (Fölsing, 1997, p. 704). He had a gift for dividing his life into separate compartments – we often see this in persons with Asperger Syndrome, the artist L. S. Lowry being an extreme example (Fitzgerald, 2005).

Narrow Interests/Obsessiveness

Physics was his great interest in life – an addiction. He "soon learned to ferret out that which might lead to the bottom of things, to disregard everything else, to disregard the multitude of things that fill the mind but detract from the essential" (Fölsing, 1997, p. 59). He wanted "to know how God created this world ... I want to know his thoughts, the rest are details" (Clarke, 1971, p. 19). A direct quest for the ultimate, as opposed to incremental building on existing knowledge, is common in scientists with Asperger Syndrome. Thus, the special theory of relativity did not refer to previous work.

In school Einstein did best at algebra, geometry, and physics, and poorly at French. Verbal descriptive subjects were not his forte. He studied algebra in elementary school and worked out Pythagoras' theorem for himself. Clearly, he was a little professor, even at school. When he first encountered classical geometry, he thought it "sufficiently wonderful that man is able at all to attain such a degree of certainty and purity in thought, as the Greeks first demonstrated in geometry" (Fölsing, 1997, p. 24).

He enrolled in the Polytechnic University in Zurich six months short of the official minimum age of 18. He "studied the masters of theoretical physics with a holy zeal at home" and avoided lectures that did not interest him, writing to his sister, "I never permitted myself any pleasure, any diversion, except that which my studies offer, keeps me upright and must protect me from despair" (Fölsing, 1997, p. 51). As a physicist, his theoretical work would provide intense experience and indescribable joy.

Einstein has been described as having an uncanny sense of the whole in scientific problems on which he was working, similar to the mode of thinking of some children with learning difficulties, who are often described as global thinkers. He was a visual thinker – a daydreamer. Persons with autism tend to be strong in the visuo-spatial realm.

Routines/Control

Einstein controlled his relationships with his family and with women mainly by neglecting them and by not allowing them to interfere with his life work. He maintained an extraordinarily intense schedule of work throughout his life.

What mattered most to him was to keep his independence. It was extremely important for him to control his own life. When learning to play the violin as a boy, his "love of music awakened only when he himself became interested in certain pieces and replaced his lessons with self-teaching" (Fölsing, 1997, p. 26). He was not interested in the advancement of his career and regarded participation in "this race of the intellects" as "a bad kind of slavery" (Fölsing, 1997, p. 626).

The man responsible for bringing Einstein to Princeton, the educationist Abraham Flexner, tried to force him to maintain a low profile, telling him that his security in America depended on his silence and rejection of all public appearances. Flexner attempted to sabotage Einstein's appearance as a violinist at a charity concert for the benefit of refugees; he also opened Einstein's mail and declined invitations on his behalf, including an invitation to the White House. Einstein rebelled against these restrictions when he found out about them; he threatened to leave Princeton, and Flexner was forced to desist.

Language/Humor

In classic autistic fashion, the young Albert's speech development proceeded slowly. His parents worried at his lack of progress and consulted a doctor. Fölsing (1997) noted that the delay seems to have been due to an early ambition to speak only in complete sentences. Every sentence he uttered, no matter how routine, he would repeat to himself softly, moving his lips. This habit persisted until his seventh year. His acquisition of language, therefore, was "laborious and self-critical … in contrast to most children's natural, unproblematical learning" (Fölsing, 1997, p. 11). He does not appear to have lacked a sense of humor.

Lack of Empathy

Einstein's younger son, Eduard, developed schizophrenia in 1932, and was admitted to Burghölzli psychiatric hospital. Einstein was a "difficult father, who would stay out of touch for months on end and then would try to forcibly to impose his will on his sons" (Fölsing, 1997, p. 671). Einstein made his final farewell to Eduard in 1933, many years before he died. He had a rather disturbing attitude to his younger son, having previously stated that "valuable individuals must not be sacrificed to hopeless things, not even in this instance" (Fölsing, 1997, p. 671). Elsa, his second wife, observed that "nothing tragic really gets to him, he is in the happy position of being able to shuffle it off. That is also why he can work so well" (Fölsing, 1997, p. 688; this related to his stepdaughter, Ilse, falling ill and dying at the age of 37).

His lack of social empathy was shown by his premature application for promotion at the patent office in Berne. He was also unsuccessful in many job applications despite his brilliant talents. Later, he showed a lack of tact in expecting others – even those with considerable professional status – to do his literature searches for him. Fölsing (1997) noted that his remarks on personal matters were often "guided less by tact or sensitivity than by ruthless frankness" (p. 69).

Naivety/Childishness

As a young man, Einstein was largely unaware of life's difficulties, and was naïve when he intimated to Mileva, in Fölsing's words (1997), that the two of them, arm in arm "would bestride the scientific stage and amaze the world" (p. 71).

He sometimes showed a certain social innocence or naivety – a lack of conventional flexibility – in his dealings with people. Later, his attachment to certain causes, such as his espousal of world government, would be regarded as naïve.

Nonverbal Communication

In the 1920s, the diplomat Count Harry Kessler noted, "The ironical trait in Einstein's facial expression, the 'Pierrot lunaire' quality, the smiling and doleful skepticism that plays around his eyes, emerges ever more strongly" (Fölsing, 1997, p. 548). He was not good at personal hygiene. In 1913, Elsa gave him a hairbrush and a toothbrush and attempted to educate him about hygiene; he eventually wrote to her "But if I begin to groom my body then I'm no longer myself ... your honestly filthy Albert" (Fölsing, 1997, p. 233).

Conclusion

Although Einstein's case is by no means clear-cut, he might meet the criteria for Asperger Syndrome (Gillberg, 1991), with the exception of a lack of information on motor problems (which is a controversial point anyway; Gillberg [1991] stated that motor clumsiness may be less a feature of persons with high-IQ Asperger Syndrome).

According to the American Psychiatric Association's (1994) DSM-IV, he would possibly meet the criteria for autism rather than Asperger Syndrome, which contentiously requires typical language development. The evidence presented here points to (high-functioning) autism or Asperger Syndrome.

CHAPTER 15

Bernard Law Montgomery
(1887–1976)

B ernard Law Montgomery
(1st Viscount
Montgomery
of Alamein)
was a prominent
British military
leader in
World War II
and its aftermath.
He became
famous for his
successful
campaigns
against the Axis

forces in Egypt, Libya, and Tunisia and was later deputy commander of NATO. He wrote several books, including his *Memoirs* (1958) and *The Path to Leadership* (1961).

In this chapter, the evidence that Field Marshal Montgomery had Asperger Syndrome or Asperger's disorder (American Psychiatric Association, 1994) is examined.

Life History

Bernard Montgomery was born on November 17, 1887, the fourth child and third son in the family. His great-uncle, Samuel Montgomery (known as Uncle Montgomery), was obsessed with religion and frittered away the family legacy. He was eccentric, lived with his two unmarried sisters, and was ignorant of the ways of the world. Samuel had a diminutive carriage built so that he would not have to give a lift to the local poor. He suffered from depression and was shy.

Robert Montgomery (Bernard's paternal grandfather), a brave soldier and a brother of Samuel Montgomery, never received due recognition for what he did, because he was not a man to push his own claims, according to Hamilton (1981). He disarmed the Sepoy Regiment when the Indian mutiny broke out and was clearly a brilliant decision maker under stress.

Montgomery's maternal grandfather, the clergyman and theological writer Frederic Farrar, was reserved and shy. He was ill at ease in company, could not make small talk, and appeared unapproachable. He tended to write for most of the day and also to spend much of the night writing or correcting proofs.

Bernard Montgomery's mother had an indomitable will and a passion for order, method, and routine (Hamilton, 1981). Very critical of her son, she was basically affectionless toward Bernard. His father, Henry, was a bishop and was completely dominated by the mother. Montgomery tended to idealize his father.

Bernard Montgomery was a wayward and immature child. He was regarded as the black sheep of the family – a troublemaker and sometimes a renegade. He was also described as charmless, mischievous, and individualist (Moorehead, 1946). The rigidity of his personality was shown when he decided to join the army: He had a tremendous argument with his mother but achieved his aim.

In school he often dreamed his way through the day. He considered work a nuisance, and his conduct in class was abysmal or sometimes strange. He had no notion of style in writing essays and was regarded as backward in mathematics, while in Latin, French, science and art he was marked no higher than "fair." He was regarded as being slow to grasp principles, self-sufficient, intolerant of authority, and steeled to take punishment, but industrious in things that interested him (Hamilton, 1981). Control was extraordinarily important to him, and on the playing fields in school he could plan his own battles. His behavior on the rugby pitch was downright violent.

In personality he was described as extremely egocentric and eccentric (Montgomery, 1987). He had an awkward, single-minded, and prickly character (Horne, 1994), and was described as a tragedy of personality and failed communications (Taylor, 1965). In the army, he was neither willing nor able to cooperate with his fellow chiefs of staff.

Possible Indicators of Asperger Syndrome

Social Behavior

As Horne (1994) pointed out, Montgomery always had problems in peer relations – in fact, he was unable to deal with his peers. He had a lifelong inability to open up to contemporaries and isolated himself from other senior officers. His lack of empathy was seen when he said that very few of his contemporaries at Staff College were any good. Horne pointed to his self-contained, solitary, awkward, unclubbable, and intractable disposition *vis-à-vis* his colleagues and his susceptibility to abrasive arrogance and intolerance. He was so isolated in his headquarters (he did not read papers sent to him) that he could not understand the criticism and jealousy that his behavior was causing among the British and U.S. Army chiefs. He described U.S. errors in the Ardennes battle with a ruthless clarity that was grossly insensitive and totally counterproductive. In addition, he was supercilious in his treatment of the U.S. military (Horne, 1994).

Generally, he was extremely poor at communicating with his superiors, such as General Eisenhower, whom he would lecture as if he were patronizing a student at Staff College (Horne, 1994). Indeed, he tended not to communicate with Eisenhower, and this caused major problems because the Americans could not understand why he was not advancing in the war more quickly, particularly at Caen – they could not understand because he did not explain it to them. He was regarded as scandalously peremptory and contemptuous and was christened Chief

Big Wind by the U.S. military establishment in Europe; indeed, Field Marshal Brooke described his relations with U.S. soldiers as a disaster (Horne, 1994).

According to Winston Churchill, Montgomery made it a rule not to accept hospitality from any of his subordinate commanders. His essential lack of sensitivity was felt not only by men but also by women, and he was described as a misogynist. He claimed that one could not marry and be an efficient officer. Kay Summersby, Eisenhower's driver, described him as a supercilious, woman-hating little martinet (Horne, 1994).

Narrow Interests/Obsessiveness

Soldiering was Montgomery's only interest. In comparison to another senior officer in the British Army, Alan Brooke, he was less practical and much narrower in his skills and interests (Brett-James, 1984).

He wanted to master his profession, and was full of energy. According to Hamilton (1981), it was Montgomery's keenness that stood out most. He had an enormous capacity for work and an imperturbable efficiency; he threw himself into his soldiering with a dedication that seemed to border on madness. Not surprisingly, he suggested a narrow strategy for ending World War II rather than a broad strategy (i.e., attacking over a broad front, which Eisenhower put forward and carried through successfully). Controversy remains as to how successful his narrow-front strategy would have been.

Routines/Control

Montgomery exerted control over both himself and others. What people especially noticed about him was his self-will: His iron determination singled him out from seemingly more talented, more educated and more appropriate leaders, according to Horne (1994). He went to bed rigidly at 9:30 p.m. and was extremely routine-bound. He was described as a man of completely regular habits and could be obstinate to the point of bigotry – he would never admit that he had altered a battle plan (Brett-James, 1984). As a result of his inflexible personality, he was not good at seizing opportunities (Horne, 1994).

Montgomery imposed tyrannical discipline on others. He was only interested in his soldiers as efficient fighting machines and looked after their health and morale for this reason only. He totally controlled the younger officers: They did not argue with him, and they were totally obedient, like all his staff had to be (Hamilton, 1981). Any sensitivity shown to junior officers was solely on the basis of his total control and their obedience (Horne, 1994).

Montgomery could be vindictive and cruel. As he grew up, he bullied other children and was beaten himself. Even during World War I, his mother appears to have regarded him as an all-too-bossy child. In midlife he had a brief marriage to a 17-year-old named Betty Anderson; once again, he controlled everything and took over her life (Horne, 1994).

Despite his egocentricity, soldiers liked to have somebody who knew what he was doing (i.e., to have a leader in full charge;

Horne, 1994). Mostly, Montgomery was an obsessively cautious commander, but on rare occasions he was capable of extreme recklessness in actions and relationships (e.g., at Arnhem and in his relationship with Eisenhower).

Language/Humor

We have no information on speech and language problems.

Lack of Empathy

Throughout his life Montgomery showed a gross lack of a capacity to empathize or understand what others might be feeling. Indeed, on one occasion he was reduced in military rank because he set fire to another cadet in military college. He had no political sense, and could not see the implications of what he was doing and how others might view his actions.

Although essentially a shy man, Montgomery showed his lack of empathy through boastfulness, vanity, and cutting out his family. He lorded it over his friends and finally became a despot (Hamilton, 1981). It appears that de Guingand, his chief of staff, was essentially a loyal subordinate but had a much wider range of human qualities than Montgomery and much greater capacity for empathy, as well as an instinctive gift for friendship and good humor that Montgomery did not have.

Montgomery's lack of sensitivity and empathy was also seen in his treatment of his son David, whom he would not allow to visit his grandmother or any other members of the family during the war. Indeed, David saw very little of his father for a period of 10 years (Horne, 1994).

Naivety/Childishness

In frontline warfare, Montgomery could concentrate on immediate tasks without worrying over other things, and was able to see things with the simple clarity of a child. This was advantageous in the fog of war (Hamilton, 1994).

Nonverbal Communication

His brother Brian Montgomery (1987) stated that a girl who was dancing with him found him stiff and unamusing. Horne (1994) noted that the atmosphere around him was one of extraordinary quietness and calm.

He showed a lack of fear during battle that can only be described as abnormal, with no trace of apprehension for his future safety. He was decorated for bravery.

Motor Clumsiness

We have no information on motor clumsiness.

Conclusion

Montgomery demonstrates a qualitative impairment in social interaction and restricted repetitive and stereotyped patterns of behavior, interests and activities. He meets the criteria for Asperger's disorder according to the DSM-IV (American Psychiatric Association, 1994) and meets the criteria for Asperger Syndrome (Gillberg, 1996) with the exception of motor clumsiness and speech and language problems.

The issue of high-functioning autism (or autistic disorder as classified in DSM-IV) also has to be considered. He meets the criteria for qualitative impairment in social interaction, as just noted. For the second criterion – qualitative impairments in communication – it is more difficult to draw a final conclusion. One can say that there is no evidence of a capacity for symbolic play in childhood, and, indeed, he was very poor at writing essays in school. He certainly had an impairment in the ability to sustain communication; as Horne (1994) pointed out, Montgomery was a lonely man. He did meet the third criterion of restricted, repetitive, and stereotyped patterns of behavior, interests, and activities. Nevertheless, Asperger Syndrome is the most likely diagnosis.

Although he had serious impairment in the capacity for empathy, it is also possible that he had problems with central coherence (Frith, 1989); that is, he was always good at taking into account his immediate battlefield in both wars, but was poor at understanding the bigger picture. The serious mistakes that he made as a result prolonged World War II (e.g., not capturing the port of Antwerp and not pursuing Rommel after the battle of Alamein). His inability to communicate with his superiors, and with Eisenhower, in particular, made him extremely unpopular in the United States and almost led to him being fired from his job.

It is difficult to know whether there was a family history of Asperger Syndrome, but there was evidence of relevant traits on both the maternal and the paternal side.

CHAPTER 16

Charles de Gaulle
(1890–1970)

De Gaulle was a colossus of twentieth-century French life – easily the most important Frenchman since Napoleon. According to Douglas Johnson (2000), "in the 1980s and 90s, opinion polls regularly showed that four out five French people, irrespective of age, sex, political opinions or socio-professional status, approved of de Gaulle. In 1995 an extended poll asked the customary sample of French voters to name their preference among the leading political personalities of the twentieth century. De Gaulle came first, easily outdistancing Martin Luther King, John Fitzgerald Kennedy, Mahatma Gandhi, John Paul II, Winston Churchill and others" (p. 3).

Life History

De Gaulle was born in Lille on November 22, 1890, the third child of Henri de Gaulle and Jeanne Maillot. His sister Marie-Agnès stated that Charles was a difficult child, who never obeyed his mother. He was described as pugnacious, unruly, and imperious. In play, "Charles was always the King of France and he always had the French army under his orders" (Lacouture, 1990, p. 7). He read an enormous amount.

Charles, a catholic, was educated by Christian Brothers and Jesuits. As a child, he amused himself by solving problems in mathematics as though they were crossword puzzles (Lacouture, 1990). He was a good historian and wrote a good deal of poetry. Early on he became obsessed by the idea of an army career. "Even in the middle of his adolescence Charles de Gaulle saw himself as the head of the armies of France" (Lacouture, 1990, p. 3). De Gaulle later wrote that at this time he felt that the whole point of life consisted of one day rendering France some conspicuous service. Lacouture (1990) described him as a "tall thin young man with a prodigious memory, a notebook crammed with aphorisms and quotations, and a habit of producing disconcerting outbursts and peremptory remarks who at the end of the summer of 1909 was feverishly waiting for the results of the entrance examination for Saint-Cyr" (an army training school) (p. 13).

De Gaulle duly attended Saint-Cyr and served with distinction in World War I. He escaped to London during the fall of France in 1940. After his forces failed to capture Dakar, he took part in the successful Allied campaigns in Syria and Madagascar. In 1958, he became prime minister and then president of France. He retired from politics in 1969, and died in 1970.

Possible Indicators of Asperger Syndrome

Social Behavior

At school de Gaulle was good at football and liked to be the referee (rather like Einstein, as we have seen). He showed his oddness and eccentricity by signing his full name in a letter to his father.

During World War I, de Gaulle's colleagues regarded him as a steel-hard character, showing an almost inhuman lack of emotion in difficult circumstances – a magnificent indifference to both terror and pain and an exceptional pride and sense of duty (Lacouture, 1990). As a prisoner of war, he tried to escape many times. He appeared unapproachable, and was said to have an unquestionable ascendancy over those around him.

He had a somewhat rebellious temperament and, like Montgomery, he had trouble with his superiors, of whom he was often contemptuous. Some of them commented on his character: General Bineau wrote that de Gaulle's gifts were mostly hidden by "a cold and lofty attitude which seems primarily a refuge. Quite mistrustful, indeed; does not put himself forward and is only very rarely unreserved" (Lacouture, 1990, p. 126). Further, Colonel Moyrand stated that he "spoils his undoubted qualities by his excessive self-confidence, his severity towards the opinions of others and his attitude of a king in exile"; General Dufieux wrote that he had "undeniable qualities which he unfortunately spoils by a somewhat detached [the general first used the word "remote" and then wrote over it] attitude and a certain amount of self-satisfaction" (Lacouture, 1990, p. 70).

Lacouture (1990) noted that "No particular friendship marked his childhood; no prophet enthralled his adolescence; no superior officer impressed him very deeply" (p. 113). This is typically autistic. At midday he lunched alone. In the evening, like Montgomery, he would often invite some of the young officers to his table. With them he would discuss Napoleon's campaigns, the prince-bishops of the seventeenth century or the medieval poets.

Franklin D. Roosevelt had a file that contained many accusations that de Gaulle wanted to be a dictator. In London he was "imperious"; Churchill found him difficult to work with and told him "I cannot look upon you as a friend ... instead of making war on Germany you have made war on England" (Lacouture, 1990, p. 368). He showed gross lack of empathy for what the British were doing to save France. He was rigid and completely unwilling or unable to make himself acceptable to Roosevelt. In Roosevelt's view, de Gaulle was selfish, rude, haughty, offensive, and distant – a man of straw. Churchill described him as a monster.

He had a sense of invulnerability and courage, and would plunge into political crowds with no regard for his own safety. He was described as the great solitary man. His remarks were often misanthropist, misogynist, and racist, especially towards Africans and Arabs, and he could be unbearably cold to people.

François Mauriac (1966) wrote: "He seems not so much hard as remote; he looks elsewhere, over our heads ... he does not waste time on pity, or on memories. He does not seek to move us ... nothing human throbbed beneath his thick armour" (p. 44) (a line from the poet Lamartine). Mauriac thought that de Gaulle and Stalin made a perfect match.

What Mauriac (1966) found on first meeting de Gaulle was "not the disdain of all other men that his enemies attribute to him, but the narrow, unbridgeable gulf between them and himself, created not by the pride of self-conscious greatness, but by the calm certainty that he is the State and, it is not too much to say, France herself." (There is a parallel here with Eamon de Valera's, "I look into my heart and I know what the Irish people want" – De Valera is also thought to have had Asperger Syndrome; see Fitzgerald, 2004). Mauriac stated, "I was sitting opposite someone who did not distinguish himself from France, who said, openly, 'I am France,' without anyone in the world saying he was mad." He also referred to "the

gulf already stretched between de Gaulle and the political parties"
(Mauriac, 1966, p. 8; this can be seen as an autistic gulf).

The issue of his distance from people recurs. For example, Mauriac (1966) commented on the distance between de Gaulle and
Churchill, de Gaulle and Roosevelt, and de Gaulle and the resistance
fighters. At a meeting of the National Committee of the Resistance
in 1944, de Gaulle "quickly passed over the entire emotional side of
the situation," whereas any other man "would have transformed this
encounter ... into an occasion for self-congratulation, for general
conciliation" (Mauriac, 1966, p. 9). De Gaulle was a man who did
not pander or flatter. According to Mauriac, he loathed sentimental-
ity and, for that reason, people felt a chill when he spoke.

Narrow Interests/Obsessiveness

De Gaulle "believed from an early age that he was a great man, and
he always acted like one ... he behaved in a way which, seeking
grandeur, invited ridicule" (Jenkins, 1993, p. 83) France, for him,
was like a princess in a fairytale or a Madonna in a fresco. Lacouture
(1990) stated, "What counts in de Gaulle's eyes, in de Gaulle, is the
France he had the madness to believe he embodied: and this madness was not a madness, but the most intense reality" (p. 191). His
passion was for France as she had been created by a thousand years
of history. He had a single focus and interest, and that was France.

As a result, he saw no other purpose in life than to leave his mark
on events. Like Ludwig Wittgenstein, he was indifferent to money.
He would "be the first man of France, or nothing – rather, the
restorer of French greatness, or nothing" (Lacouture, 1990, p. 27;

again, there are parallels with de Valera). Inherited or acquired opinions played no part in his position.

In another instance of obsessiveness, he had a mania for chronology. For a quarter of a century de Gaulle "tirelessly hammered in the same nails again and again, repeated the same ideas in the hope – ultimately rewarded, at least in the constitutional realm – of translating them into facts" (Mauriac, 1966, p. 99).

Routines/Control

Not surprisingly, de Gaulle always wanted to be close to the centers of decision, where he could exert maximum control. Control is central to persons with high-functioning autism. At military school, he belonged to the swots, and attempted to "learn in order to conquer" – the motto of Saint-Cyr (Lacouture, 1990).

He went into the infantry, possibly, according to Lacouture (1990), because of an impulse for austerity and renunciation. He was decorated during World War I and was undoubtedly extremely brave and calm under fire, not unlike Ludwig Wittgenstein or Montgomery. Lacouture (1990) described him as "the tireless pursuer of soup-eating sentinels, the giver of dictatorial lessons, the captain-who-remains-standing-under-the-shrapnel, the mixture of Cyrano and Horatius who always seemed to want to make poor mortals ashamed of being merely men" (p. 37). In command he drove his forces relentlessly both day and night in training exercises.

Consistent with this tendency, in 1927 de Gaulle stated, "such as I am, I cannot fail to be, at a given moment, in the centre of the stage"

(Mauriac, 1966, p. 16). Later, he was often accused of an implacable impulse to dominate at all costs and was suspected of having dictatorial ambitions. He never acknowledged making a mistake.

De Gaulle wrote in 1927, that "in any event, a leader of this quality is inevitably aloof, for there can be no authority without prestige, and no prestige unless he keeps his distance" (Mauriac, 1966, p. 18; again this reminds one of the "distance" associated with autism). Even as a young man, Mauriac (1966) noted, he was "already determined not to please, to remain alone, not out of misanthropy or because he was so inclined but because domination implies solitude" (p. 18).

Mauriac (1966) noted that in 1954 "No one dreams of asking him: 'Have you the government's consent?' This is because, by his mere presence, General de Gaulle makes the lilliputian dictatorship invisible to the naked eye" (p. 36) (this reminds one of de Valera). To those whose profession was politics, de Gaulle seemed "the incarnation of all that was most hateful: the absolute preponderance of the State, the cult of the nation, the indifference to ideologies, the mistrust of political parties, plus an antagonism to them personally and the determination to dominate, to defy, and, if possible, to destroy them" (Mauriac, 1966, p. 10).

De Gaulle withdrew from government in January 1946, and was in the wilderness for a very long time – probably much longer than he had expected (not unlike de Valera). He had to withdraw because the political parties had made government impossible for him. "He was withdrawing only to break the threads by which the Lilliputians had bound him and to create the conditions of his return 'as master'"

(Mauriac, 1966, p. 35). De Gaulle did not anticipate that France could do without him for more than a few days, but he was mistaken. In a way he was a dictator in the manner of de Valera (it is interesting that he met de Valera in Dublin after leaving office in France); i.e., "one who finally, and by his own means, imposed his Constitution, his foreign policy, and everything he believed, even if he was the only man in France who believed it" (Mauriac, 1966, p. 143).

The instructions he gave for his funeral were extraordinarily detailed, again showing his penchant for control. He insisted that no president, minister, or representative of parliament or any other corporate body be allowed to attend.

Language/Humor

According to Douglas Johnson (2000), "de Gaulle, it is argued, is not a great literary figure. His style, with its classical echoes, its aspiration to achieve a certain monumentalism and its repetitions, is theoretical rather than dramatic" (p. 3). He retains an autistic repetitiveness.

Further, "as soon as de Gaulle opens his mouth, one hears the same sovereign tone" (voice of Asperger Syndrome?). In his lectures he showed "shafts of iconoclastic wit" (Mauriac, 1966).

As a teacher of army people, he showed an "abrupt and sometimes flowing eloquence" (Lacouture, 1990, p. 64). As early as 1921, at Saint-Cyr, "he would gaze at the audience in a way peculiar to himself. Immensely tall, upright, with his stiff collar tight round his over-long neck, he would talk for two solid hours without looking at his notes ... [he had] extraordinary ascendancy over men of all ages and all ranks" (Lacouture, 1990, p. 64). This is similar to Ludwig Wittgenstein and a feature of high-functioning autism.

De Gaulle's *Mémoires* are typical autistic memoirs. They are good as collections of facts but lack a sense of the individual writing them (i.e., the unknown person who must have suffered, who must have loved and been loved). Persons with autism have problems with narrative.

Naivety/Childishness

According to Jenkins (1993), de Gaulle believed that gratitude had no place in the relations of statesmen. He was hostile to all the efforts after the war that Britain and the United States made on his behalf and on behalf of France. He "bit the British hand which fed him" (p. 3). After the Germans had overrun France early in World War II, he stated, "France is a great power" (Jenkins, 1993, p. 89). This was ridiculous at the time.

Nonverbal Communication

De Gaulle was extremely punctual, and "trapped in time like a mammoth in ice," according to Claude Dulong (Lacouture, 1990, p. 236). Dulong stated that de Gaulle had moments of idleness that surprised everybody: "Sometimes he was seen *doing nothing*. He might be sitting on a chair or standing behind his desk, perfectly erect and motionless, his hands placed in front of him, flat on the wood. A megalith. In those moments, he was reminiscent of a Henry Moore statue, particularly one of them, The King. He had to be in the grip of some torment to pace up and down his office with long, stiff, slight swaying steps, his hands behind his back, passing in front of one of the windows to turn his eyes on the rather small garden" (Lacouture, 1990, pp. 236–237).

Lacouture (1990) recalled the words of one of de Gaulle's secretaries: "He wore a bowler hat and he carried a stick and he always looked preoccupied. As he walked he looked up into the sky and waved his stick as though he were writing in the air" (p. 78). This is similar to Ludwig Wittgenstein.

Narcissism and Grandiosity

In a clear example of grandiosity, de Gaulle wrote in 1929, "In a few years, people will be clinging to my coattails to save the country," noted Mauriac (1966, p. 13). Emmanuel de Astier, who knew de Gaulle in London, described a meeting with him:

> It did not matter that he was only the leader of a handful of men and a few remote territories; his enemies and his pride had increased him to such a size that he spoke as though he bore a thousand years of history within him or as though he were standing back for a century and seeing himself written in it. He drew a dark picture of his Calvary – that of France in person. And it suddenly occurred to me that he was giving himself up to this black fervour purely to stimulate the genius of France to recover its national and historic power, the only one he believed in. Although he was capable of drawing so much wisdom from a piece of madness, he perceived nothing but empiricism. He so thoroughly embod-

ied the nation, he so wholly felt himself to be the nation that he forgot the people in it and the immediate present and the incoherence and the necessary Utopia and that remote future which is called mankind. How could one tell him of it? There is no arguing with a Symbol about that which he symbolizes. (Lacouture, 1991, p. 486)

According to Mauriac (1996), "If the general, speaking of himself, often says 'De Gaulle' this is because he regards himself from outside, in the timeless light of history" (p. 157). When Paris was liberated, he described himself as not a person but an instrument of destiny. This had been an element of his self-image since his youth.

He created turmoil when he visited Montreal in 1967, with a peroration that consisted of exclamations: "Vive Montréal! Vive le Québec! Vive le Québec libre! Vive la Canada française et vive la France!" (Lacouture, 1991, p. 455). Inflaming passions in French-speaking Quebec, de Gaulle showed a lack of empathy for the people of Canada and was interfering in internal politics.

Motor Skills

De Gaulle did poorly in musketry in military school, possibly because he did not have good motor skills.

Conclusion

Charles de Gaulle showed most of the traits necessary to support a diagnosis of Asperger Syndrome. He is reminiscent of two other political leaders – President Eamon de Valera of Ireland and President Thomas Jefferson of the United States – who also showed signs of Asperger Syndrome. De Gaulle was enigmatic and extremely controlling, with a lack of empathy in social relations, a lack of capacity for social reciprocity, and a tendency to repetitive talk – he talked at people rather than to them and had a preoccupied look.

CHAPTER 17

Alfred C. Kinsey
(1894–1956)

The pioneering American sexologist Alfred Kinsey was born on June 23, 1894, in Hoboken, New Jersey. He was educated at Bowdoin College and Harvard University, and became a professor of zoology at Indiana

University. Here he conducted a major study of the taxonomy of gall wasps and wrote several books on zoology and botany, including *Edible Wild Plants of Eastern North America*. In 1921, he married Clara McMillen; they had four children, of whom the first, Bruce, died at the age of 2.

In order to investigate human sexual behavior scientifically, Kinsey founded the Institute for Sex Research at Indiana University in 1942. His findings, based on interviews with 18,000 men and women, were published in two controversial books: *Sexual Behavior in the Human Male* (1948) and *Sexual Behavior in the Human Female* (1953). Kinsey died of heart disease on August 25, 1956, in Bloomington, Indiana.

Kinsey's name is synonymous with sex research, but what has not been commented on previously is that he met more than likely the criteria for Asperger Syndrome. He had major problems in social relationships throughout his life, and particular problems related to empathy. He showed continuous difficulties in social and emotional reciprocity and was regarded as aloof, dominating, and a loner. He had very restricted interests in biology and music. His scientific contribution was limited by his weak central coherence. That is, while he showed an enormous capacity for collecting facts, he was unable to theorize or to integrate these facts into a bigger picture. Nevertheless, his contribution to sex research was enormous. It is interesting to see certain Asperger-type traits, such as restricted interests, being of use in furthering human knowledge.

The genetic and environmental environment of every great man (see Note 10) plays a part in his greatness and in the choice of topic that he chooses to research. Every human being has a dark side, and Kinsey was no exception.

Family and Childhood

Alfred C. Kinsey was the first child of Alfred Seguine Kinsey and Sarah Charles, who married in 1892. His father rose from a shopboy position to become a mechanical engineer. Many fathers of persons with Asperger Syndrome worked as engineers or in similar occupations. Kinsey's mother was described as having a withdrawn personality. Jones (1997) pointed out that Kinsey's father had major problems with empathy and was "a hard man who imposed his will on others with ruthless finality, dominating everyone over whom he had authority, both in the workplace and at home": basically a "tyrannical, puritan father" and a dictator, whose students greatly disliked him (pp. 19–21).

Kinsey suffered serious illness as a child: rickets, rheumatic fever, and typhoid fever. Hoboken, where he was born and grew up, was "a dingy, dirty, crowded city, one that Kinsey desperately wished to escape" (Jones, 1997, p. 13).

Possible Indicators of Asperger Syndrome

Social Behavior

Kinsey showed classical Asperger traits starting in early life. He was described as "a real serious guy. Great on books ... He was always reading. He wasn't a guy who would socialize. He was studying all the time" (Jones, 1997, p. 31). Not surprisingly, after high school he didn't keep in close contact with his classmates or any of his former teachers (except his biology teacher, Natalie Roeth). During his adolescence, "he did not make a single close friend, at least not in the sense of having a 'best friend,' nor did he form a single friendship that extended into adulthood" (Jones, 1997, p. 33). Most people found him cold and aloof. He was described as a loner who never played ball with his classmates, was bullied, did not take part in team sports, and "just wasn't one of the guys" (Jones, 1997, pp. 48–49).

One of Kinsey's classmates, Hazel Balch, noticed in 1912, "He never fit in right" and "He wasn't the type you would go out and have a pleasant time with. If you wanted to talk bugs maybe, but he didn't have fun." He was "very serious in everything." Another classmate described him as "the shyest guy around girls you could think of" (Jones, 1997, pp. 65–66).

In college Kinsey's social life never got off the ground – "True to his pattern, he had trouble fitting in" and he was described again as a "shy and reserved" person, who "stalked about the campus with little to say to anyone"; the college newspaper advised that if he would "loosen up" he would "make quite a man" (Jones, 1997, p. 121). He took no part in most social occasions.

"Unsure of himself socially, ill at ease with others, Kinsey found it virtually impossible to make small talk. And that explains, at least in part, why he peppered people with facts" (Jones, 1997, p. 122). His inability to make small talk persisted throughout his life. Nevertheless, it appears he wanted to fit in, as many persons with Asperger Syndrome do.

The same pattern was evident throughout his graduate school years: "Kinsey was cut off from his peers, continuing the pattern of social isolation that had dogged him earlier" (Jones, 1997, p. 133). In Harvard his "social life was sparse" and he remained a "loner, a straitlaced young man whose puritanical demeanor stayed visibly in place" (p. 140). He was, again, noted to be cut off from people, isolated, aloof, and difficult to make contact with.

When he finally got a girlfriend (Clara, his future wife), instead of something personal, he bought her a compass, a hunting knife, and a pair of hiking shoes as a Christmas gift, probably not a surprising choice by a person with Asperger Syndrome.

Narrow Interests/Obsessiveness

Kinsey's colleagues Robert Yerkes and George Corner found that Kinsey had "a peculiar personality": They had never encountered anyone "so frightfully focused, so suspicious and contemptuous of the work and the opinions of others, and so unnervingly sure of himself" (Jones, 1997, p. 437).

Kinsey became fascinated with classification in biology and went into taxonomy, becoming an entomologist. He showed the classical single-minded devotion to his studies, which placed him at odds with most students at the university.

Similar traits were found in other areas of his life. When Kinsey took up gardening, he had to have "the very best iris collection in the whole midwest" (Jones, 1997, p. 249). He also collected music records. In his second career as a sexologist, the collecting impulse again took over. As Jones pointed out, Kinsey's fondness for numbers spilled over into his new area of research.

He was unable to relax completely in his early professional life (and later), had no interest in reading novels, and was largely interested only in collecting insects. He spent 20 years of his life focused on American Cynipidae (gall wasps). These are tiny insects, no larger than a small ant. Kinsey examined and measured 152,000 of them (an interesting parallel is Darwin's colossal research on tiny barnacles). Because of his obsession with collecting, he was given the nickname "get a million Kinsey" (Jones, 1997, p. 222).

The psychologist Karl S. Lashley expressed reservations about what he considered Kinsey's mindless pursuit of numbers. In 1941 Kinsey told a colleague that he planned to collect 20,000 sexual case histories – a figure that he would later raise to 100,000. Kinsey drove himself extremely hard: He worked into the early hours of the morning, and "nothing else in the world seemed to matter except the work before him. He even begrudged the time it took to eat" (Jones, 1997, p. 473). However, Jones (1997) notes that "Kinsey was not a great taxonomist, largely because he was not a great theorist ... he fell victim to his need for order and control ... Compulsive and driven, he could not stop classifying, and, ultimately, his personality vitiated his science" (p. 230).

Routines/Control

As a boy, Kinsey had "filled many lonely hours at the piano honing his skills. He showed a singular aptitude for practice, attacking the piano with the discipline, tenacity, and self-sacrifice that became his trademarks in life" (Jones, 1997, p. 35). Like many people with Asperger Syndrome, he possessed considerable musical ability, but did not pursue a musical career because he "had to be the best at everything he did," and he knew he was not a brilliant musician (Jones, 1997, p. 37).

In the 1920s and 1930s, Kinsey would invite students and colleagues to his home to hear him play the piano. Before playing each piece, he would give them a lecture on the composer. At least one student found the experience oppressively stilted, and came away feeling hurt and humiliated. Later he changed to playing records at these gatherings. Everything was planned in detail beforehand, and the visitors had to listen to him and his choice of records. Every guest was "policed into polite passivity," with Kinsey dominating (Jones, 1997, p. 253).

His rigidity and obsessionality were also evident in that these "musicales" began at 8 p.m. sharp, and ended at 10.30 p.m. on the dot. Kate Mueller, dean of women at the university, commented that Kinsey behaved like a dictator at the one session that she and her husband attended; Henry Remak, a professor of German, described the evening as "much too formal, much too frozen, much too strict for my liking" – he felt "somewhat horrified and never went back again" (Jones, 1997, pp. 254–255). Kinsey was oblivious to such reactions. With his chronic need for control, he could never give himself over entirely to the music but rather analyzed it from every conceivable angle. It was clear that he wanted distance, not absorption and control, not surrender.

When he joined the university's teaching staff at Bloomington, "Almost from the moment he set foot on campus, Kinsey struck people as headstrong, willful, stubborn, and highly opinionated ...

From the outset, Kinsey thought he knew everything about teaching" (Jones, 1997, pp. 179–180). Jones (1997) noted that Kinsey's stubborn streak ... reflected his need for control" (p. 185). Even in the publication of his books on sexual behavior, "From the outset his thinking was guided by a single issue – control" (Jones, 1997, p. 542), as he undertook the publicity role that was normally the province of the publisher.

In 1942, Kinsey's young assistant, Clyde Martin, planned to marry. When told of this, Kinsey's response was "Fine, but it will have to be done in our garden" (Jones, 1997, p. 469). At Kinsey's insistence, the couple switched the wedding from August to May – the month Kinsey's garden was at its best.

When Kinsey's sampling methods were criticized after the publication of *Sexual Behavior in the Human Male*, it was feared that his rigid personality might prevent him from addressing his critics in a constructive fashion. He had the characteristic rigidity of Asperger Syndrome and was perceived as unwilling to make changes. He harbored "very fixed and determined ideas about his own work" (Jones, 1997, p. 647). When researching *Sexual Behavior in the Human Female*, "his quest for absolute dominion over his subject matter approached megalomania" (Jones, 1997, p. 682).

Language/Humor

It was said of Kinsey that "only when he was aroused by something about which he felt very deeply were there strident overtones in his mellifluous speech" (Jones, 1997, p. 141). He was a stickler for correct pronunciation and chided students for their midwestern mode of speech, apparently oblivious to his own eastern accent. It seems that he had little or no sense of humor.

Lack of Empathy

After Kinsey became a sex researcher, he was away from home more and more. As a result, Clara saw less and less of him and felt abandoned. However, Kinsey was too busy to notice her feelings, and possibly lacked the ability to empathize with her. Helen Nowlis, the wife of a colleague, sensed "something odd in Kinsey, something that gave her pause" (Jones, 1997, p. 490).

Having submitted his lectures for a marriage course for the faculty to review, he remained "impervious to their comments": Dr. Edith Schuman stated that her impression was that "nothing ever reached him" (Jones, 1997, p. 326).

Kinsey came under pressure in 1940, after it was suggested that he had been exploiting students for his own purposes. He failed to treat warnings as wakeup calls, and badly underestimated his critics' resolve. In response to the question, "How could Kinsey have overestimated his support among the faculty so badly?" Jones (1997) answered: "For the last two years, he had lived in a fool's paradise" (p. 410). This "cut-offness" is characteristic of Asperger Syndrome.

Kinsey's lack of empathy was also shown when Corner, the chairman of the Committee on Research in Problems of Sex, invited him home for supper. The evening was a disaster: Instead of treating it as a social occasion, Kinsey "monopolized the conversation with a nonstop monologue on his research" (Jones, 1997, p. 461), which stunned both Corner's wife and daughter.

As a young professor, Kinsey immediately went "his own way" and struck people "by his headstrong, willful, stubborn, and highly opinionated" behavior; he refused "to defer to his senior colleagues and insisted on speaking his mind" (Jones, 1997, p. 183). It is hardly surprising that his criticism of colleagues made him unpopular and isolated him from staff and students. Additionally, he could not empathize with students and was excessively critical of them.

His problem with empathy was also seen in his difficulty in understanding the damage that children suffered from pedophilia: He collected vast amounts of data from predatory pedophiles, and characterized the victims as "partners" (Jones, 1997, p. 512). His assistant Wardell Pomeroy commented that Kinsey "would have done business with the devil himself if it would have furthered the research" (Jones, 1997, p. 513).

Naivety/Childishness

As a sophomore, Kinsey gave solo piano performances at concerts, giving a lecture about the piece before playing it. Other performers regarded this as very odd, but Kinsey had no idea that this was so (as we have seen, similar behavior persisted into adulthood). When he went to college, he attached himself to Professor Alfred Gross. He often arrived at Gross's home, entered the house, and played classical music on the piano before Gross and his family even woke in the morning.

Finally, Jones (1997) makes various references to Kinsey's "almost childlike faith," "childlike wonder," and "oversimplified thinking" (pp. 212, 375, 587).

Conclusion

We have no information about speech and language problems or motor clumsiness in Kinsey's case. Gillberg (1991) initially regarded both as important, but neither is necessary for a diagnosis of Asperger's disorder. He, therefore, met all but two of Gillberg's criteria. He also showed associated characteristics including paranoia and grandiosity.

Kinsey would meet the DSM-IV criteria for Asperger's disorder (American Psychiatric Association, 1994). He showed a qualitative impairment in social interaction, with a failure to develop appropriate peer relationships and lack of social and emotional reciprocity. He could only share with people when they were interested in what interested him (i.e., biology, sex, or music). He showed a pattern of restricted and repetitive interests and activities that was abnormal in intensity and focus. He was rigid and inflexible.

Clearly high achievement is possible with Asperger's disorder. Indeed, the focus on a narrow interest can have scientific advantages to the researcher and produce a great deal of new knowledge, as Kinsey did in the area of the sexual behavior of Americans.

CHAPTER 18

Norbert Wiener
(1894–1964)

The American mathematician Norbert Wiener was the founder of cybernetics. A mathematical prodigy, he studied zoology at Harvard and philosophy at Cornell; between 1919 and 1960 he served as assistant professor and then professor of mathematics at the Massachusetts Institute of Technology.

During World War II, Wiener's work involved him in automatic computing, mathematical communication theory, and feedback theory. This in turn led him to draw comparisons between the handling of information by electronic devices and by animals, which led in turn to the emergence of the field of cybernetics.

Life History

Norbert Wiener was born on November 26, 1894, into a Jewish family in Columbia, Missouri. His father was "a very intelligent and independent young man" and an unusual person – an autodidact who spoke several languages by the age of 13, and who became a professor of Slavic languages at Harvard (Levinson, 1966, p. 2). According to Levinson, Norbert was "a timid anxious child who was sustained by the 'solicitude and tenderness,' to use his words, of his mother." Norbert described his father as "brilliant, absent-minded and hot-tempered"; Levinson believed that these adjectives also applied to Norbert (p. 2).

Norbert had a "markedly unconventional personality, his mother tried to smooth over some of the rough spots but to no avail" (Levinson, 1966, p. 2). According to Levinson (1966), "Norbert learned to read spontaneously at a very early age and also picked up arithmetic. Already by six he was reading the widest variety of books in his father's library" (p. 3). He was attracted to zoology, physics, and chemistry. One article he read as a child excited in him "the desire to devise quasi-living automata" (Levinson, 1966, p. 3). He was fascinated by the imagination of H. G. Wells. Like many other geniuses, such as Einstein, as a child Wiener was not interested in learning by rote at school.

He was educated at Tufts College and at Cornell, Harvard, Cambridge, Göttingen, and Columbia universities and became professor of mathematics at the Massachusetts Institute of Technology. In 1926 he married Margaret Engelmann, a woman who would "require tact, forbearance, and a willingness to assume almost all family responsibility, to shelter Norbert from outside distractions, to humor him when depressed, to allay his fears and anxiety, and to tolerate him in his unbounded flights of fancy when he was cheerful" (Levinson, 1966, p. 22). This reminds us of the wives of Gödel, Einstein, Hilbert, and others; it sounds like a typical "autistic marriage." He needed a great deal of reassurance about his work from those around him.

Wiener wrote several books on his theories and his life in the 1940s, 1950s, and 1960s.

Work

During World War II, Wiener researched on anti-aircraft defense techniques and tried to produce a mathematical and electronic system for communicating vital information. He became interested in automatic computing and feedback theory. He thus founded the science of cybernetics – the general theory of control and communication in machines, animals, and organizations. The idea of a "thinking machine" is a common autistic interest; Wiener set about devising a systematic mathematical theory that would be capable of underpinning such a machine.

Possible Indicators of Asperger Syndrome

Social Behavior

Wiener was socially an undeveloped and inept child. At Columbia University, "his sharp tongue and lack of social sensitivity made him something of a nuisance and accordingly he was treated badly by the graduate students in the dormitory in which he lived" (Levinson, 1966, p. 9). He later said, "I had no proper idea of personal cleanliness and personal neatness, and I myself never knew when I was to blurt out some unpardonable rudeness or *double entendre*" (Levinson, 1966, p. 149). He described himself as a lone wolf.

During the war he became a reserve officer and was "shocked by [his tent mates'] drinking and swearing. Once his tent mates realized how sensitive he was, they taunted him mercilessly. Needless to say, he was not judged to be officer material on the finishing camp" (Levinson, 1966, p. 11).

In his teaching, "he was inexperienced and almost certainly inept in presenting the elementary courses assigned him. He was younger than his years, over-reactive, nervous and an easy victim to baiting. The students made his life miserable" (Levinson, 1966, p. 11). Whereas Ludwig Wittgenstein was extremely unsympathetic and ungrateful to Bertrand Russell, Wiener was equally ungrateful to a mentor he had at Harvard – a mathematician called Kellogg.

Narrow Interests/Obsessiveness

Wiener undoubtedly developed a compulsive obsession and passion for his mathematical work.

Routines/Control

Wiener was "a combative and fascinating conversationalist, although with his great intellectual power and aggressiveness it was difficult for him to limit his share in a discussion" (Levinson, 1966, p. 18).

There is a (possibly apocryphal) story about Wiener's absent-mindedness and his adherence to routine, which recalls an anecdote regarding David Hilbert (see Chapter 11). After they moved house, Wiener's wife was aware that on leaving work he would forget that he should go to the new house. According to Devlin (2000),

> She handed him a slip of paper with his new address, realizing that by evening he would forget it. By evening, of course, Wiener was deeply engrossed in mathematical thought and absent-mindedly walked to his old home. As he headed up the garden path he suddenly remembered that he was supposed to go to the new house. But what was the address? He began to search his pockets for the slip of paper his wife had pressed into his hands that morning. Where was it? There were dozens of slips of paper in his pockets, most of them covered with

mathematics. Just then he noticed a child sitting on the porch of his old home. "Little girl," he said, "do you know where the people who used to live here have gone?" The girl looked up at him and smiled. "Yes Daddy, of course I do. Mummy said you would go to the wrong home and would lose the address, so she sent me to fetch you." (pp. 126–127)

While Wiener's daughter does not support this story, she did acknowledge that he was extremely absent-minded (Devlin, 2000).

Language/Humor

Wiener was proficient in most of the languages of Western Europe, and had a limited conversational ability in Chinese. He loved to use these languages. Persons with autism spectrum disorders often have special linguistic ability.

Naivety/Childishness

From the biographical information, it is clear that Wiener was capable of child-like egocentric immaturity (although he was equally capable of extreme idealism and generosity).

Motor Clumsiness

As a child, he was very poor at laboratory work and probably clumsy in that he lacked manipulative skill. He later said that he had been "clumsier than the run of children around me. Some of this clumsiness was genuinely poor muscular co-ordination, but more of it was based on my defective eyesight" (Levinson, 1966, p. 74).

Also, his mechanical clumsiness in writing "tended to make me omit any word that I could eliminate, and to force me into a great crabbiness of style" (Levinson, 1966, p. 104). He ascribed his tendency towards impatience to "a combination of mental quickness and physical slowness" (Levinson, 1966, p. 128).

Anxiety/Depression

According to Levinson (1996), Wiener's insecurity caused him to believe that the Harvard mathematics professors were looking down at the students, including himself. Persons with autism spectrum disorder often have paranoid aspects to their character.

Idiosyncrasies

He was viewed as an eccentric at Cambridge University. At the Massachusetts Institute of Technology, Wiener's "eccentricities were not regarded as out of place in a college teacher and indeed the students seemed pleased to have at least one teacher who could not be mistaken for anything else except a budding college professor" (Levinson, 1966, p. 13).

Conclusion

Norbert Wiener appears to have displayed most or all of the characteristics associated with Asperger Syndrome.

CHAPTER 19

Charles A. Lindbergh
(1902–1974)

Charles Augustus Lindbergh was born on February 4, 1902, in Detroit. In 1927, he gained worldwide fame as the first person to make a nonstop solo transatlantic flight when he flew from

New York to Paris, where he was greeted by 150,000 people. Lindbergh made many other long-distance flights, but his fame was tainted by his admiration for Nazi Germany in the 1930s and his insistence that the United States should stay out of World War II (although he worked for the U.S. Air Force during the war and flew some combat missions).

In 1929 Lindbergh married Anne Morrow, daughter of the U.S. ambassador to Mexico. She later became a successful writer. The couple were subjected to intense attention in 1932, when their infant son Charles was kidnapped and murdered (Bruno Hauptmann was executed for the crime in 1936). The couple had five additional children.

Alexis Carrel of the Rockefeller Institute, a French surgeon who worked with Lindbergh to develop an artificial heart pump, described him as a great savant. Lindbergh made enormous accomplishments in various fields; his intellectual hunger was vast. He was a researcher and innovator always at the cutting edge. He died in Hawaii in August 1974.

Lindbergh showed some unusual traits, which we believe may be ascribed to Asperger Syndrome.

Family and Childhood

Lindbergh's paternal grandfather, Ola Månsson, was a politician and banker who had to leave Sweden because of illegal banking activities. He, his second wife, and baby son (Lindbergh's father) settled in Minnesota, where father and baby became August Lindbergh and Charles August Lindbergh. "Combating adversity with stoicism, August Lindbergh established the work ethic his descendants would emulate" (Berg, 1998, p. 7).

C. A. Lindbergh practiced as an attorney and was elected to Congress. After his first wife died at the age of 30, leaving two daughters, he married Evangeline Lodge – a science teacher and the daughter of two of Detroit's most prominent families – in 1901. They had one child: Charles Lindbergh.

The marriage was an unhappy one. Evangeline had a reputation for wild temper tantrums and wilder spending habits, and for constant nagging; C. A. was unfaithful. They lived apart from 1909. Lindbergh's family history included "financial malfeasance, flight from justice, bigamy, illegitimacy, melancholia, manic-depression, alcoholism, grievous generational conflicts, and wanton abandonment of families" (Berg, 1998, p. 25).

Possible Indicators of Asperger Syndrome

Social Behavior

As a young boy Lindbergh was taught at home by his mother, and he did not start school until he was almost 8 years of age. Later he disliked the numerous schools he attended as the family moved around, later writing that "I did not find much friendship among the children there. I did not understand them, nor they me" (Berg,

1998, p. 42). Indeed, many of the children made fun of his name, nicknaming him "Limburger" or sometimes "Cheese." He suffered from loneliness and was never part of a group of buddies. It was noted that he was painfully shy. He became a rugged individualist like his father, and chronically restless.

In an art gallery, the young Charles was especially drawn to Hiram Powers's *The Greek Slave*, a white marble statue of a naked girl in shackles, which may have resonated with something in himself. When he went to Redondo Union High School in California, "he made no friends ... sticking to himself, his family, and his dog, in the small cottage they rented on the beach" (Berg, 1998, p. 47). At Little Falls High School, Minnesota, he did well only in physics and mechanical drawing. Few of his classmates ever spoke to him, and he did not attend social functions. Similarly, at the University of Wisconsin, where he studied mechanical engineering, he felt like a fish out of water and "steered clear of most people, armouring his insecurity in an attitude of aloofness" (Berg, 1998, p. 55). He had no relationships with women at college and avoided tobacco and alcohol. In his army class he became "a chameleon, able to blend into any environment – to be a part of any group but always apart" (Berg, 1998, p. 77). He had no close friends.

After his transatlantic flight, Lindbergh became the first person to be constantly stalked by the media. He experienced this unwelcome fame alone, finding personal relationships difficult: "Solitude seemed the most he could wish for, and that would have to be a hard-fought achievement" (Berg, 1998, p. 176).

He was slow in getting involved with women because "you had to learn to dance, to talk their language, to escort them properly to restaurants and theatres." However, he grew lonely and set out to marry and start a family (late in life he wrote about what he had sought in a mate: "good health, good form, good sight and hearing" (Berg, 1998, p. 193). He was linked romantically with Elisabeth Morrow but fell in love with her shy sister, Anne (who wrote that she was "swept away by the force of his personality"), and they subsequently married.

When baby Charles was born in June 1930, Lindbergh was too frightened of the baby to have any physical contact with him. He also had difficulty playing with children. Naturally, the kidnapping and death of the child upset him enormously.

Narrow Interests/Obsessiveness

In the course of his life, Charles Lindbergh had a wide range of interests, some of which became obsessions. As a child, he indulged in solitary pursuits and became an ardent collector of "stones, arrowheads, cigar bands, coins, stamps, guns, lead soldiers, marbles, cigarette cards – almost anything he could find and stash under one of the attic eaves. And he became an inveterate maker of lists, constantly updating accounts of his possessions, as though taking an inventory of himself through his things. He was happiest alone, outside, as one with nature" (Berg, 1998, p. 40). He became interested in "the wonders of science, a world of logic and intellect," and came to believe that "science is the key to all mystery" (Berg, 1998, pp. 40–41).

Lindbergh also had a strong interest in motorcycles, and after his first flight in 1922, he became transfixed by flying. Determined to fly from New York to Paris alone, he first set about raising the money and then did a great deal of work on the plane to make sure he had the best possible chance of succeeding. He was meticulous and obsessive in his preparation; the press gave him nicknames such as the "Flyin' Fool" (Berg, 1998, p. 108).

Throughout his marriage to Anne, he was constantly traveling. He was fascinated by archaeology and studied it; he also studied rocketry and worked with Alexis Carrel on the development of a device that could pump blood if the heart was being operated upon. This later became known as an artificial heart. He also served as a human guinea pig in an aero-medical laboratory, thus contributing greatly to the development of high-altitude flying.

Lindbergh later became obsessed with the Cold War, to such an extent that his mother-in-law regarded him as a madman. He also got involved with wildlife and conservation issues, to which he devoted enormous energy. He was also obsessed with "improving the quality of life for future generations" (Berg, 1998, p. 529).

Charles Lindbergh died of cancer of the lymphatic system, having left extremely detailed instructions on all aspects of his burial and funeral service (like Charles de Gaulle).

Routines/Control

Military-style life suited Lindbergh well. The only aspect of university life that interested him was the Reserve Officer Training Corps program: "He looked forward to the 'discipline of the hour-long drills.' During the summer vacation he did six weeks of field artillery training, where 'each regulation and command made him feel he had at last found his niche. He delighted in the detailed ritual, enjoying this perpetual quest for precision" (Berg, 1998, p. 60).

Although in some respects he was a model father, Lindbergh was inclined to rule by intimidation, and the household relaxed during his absences. According to his mother-in-law, he had to control everything in the house. He imposed precise duties on his wife, including the keeping of household books and inventories of every item they possessed.

He was extraordinarily perfectionistic, especially when writing books. Charles Scribner, the publisher of his autobiography, *The Spirit of St Louis*, described him as the most fussy author he had ever encountered, and obsessed with detail.

Language/Humor

Lindbergh's sense of humor was generally expressed through practical jokes, which could be rather crude and extreme, as he never knew when to stop.

In his freshman year in college he failed English, and some of his papers were downgraded because of bad grammar. He wished that he could stop taking English and exclusively study aeronautical engineering. However, later in his life he showed a sufficiently high degree of literary skill to win the Pulitzer Prize (for *The Spirit of St Louis*). One of his editors was very moved by his descriptions of sea, air, cloud and sky. An earlier book, *Of Flight and Life*, had evoked mild astonishment among critics at the quality of Lindbergh's prose.

Lack of Empathy

Particularly in the early years, Lindbergh admired the Germany that Hitler had created; he even received the Service Cross of the German Eagle from Hermann Goering in Berlin in October 1938. This caused him enormous problems later, particularly with the Jewish community in the United States, who thought that he had not been sufficiently sympathetic to them. He seemed to have a blind spot for Nazi anti-Semitism: He could not empathize with the suffering the Jews were experiencing in Germany. In America, some referred to Lindbergh as a doomsayer, a Nazi dupe, even a collaborator. Soon he would be called "a sombre cretin," a man "without human feeling," and "the Lone Ostrich" (Berg, 1998, pp. 397, 409; he had previously been idealized as "the Lone Eagle").

Lindbergh was totally against the United States entering World War II, and "preached his beliefs with messianic fervour" (Berg, 1998, p. 7); he had great difficulty getting involved with the U.S. war effort because the government did not want him to be involved due to his lack of empathy for the official position of the United States when it became involved directly in the war.

He "buried his head in the sand when confronted with the crimes of inhumanity that repelled so many others" in Germany, and saw the USSR as the greatest long-term threat: a view that would prove correct in some respects (Berg, 1998, p. 397). Yet he was as naïve in war as he had been in peace, seeking government employment on the basis that his difference in outlook would make him of more value rather than less. More than 30 years later, he still "refused to recant anything" (Berg, 1998, p. 545).

Naivety/Childishness

Lindbergh was very much a practical joker. His naivety in wartime has also been noted. When he was courting Anne Morrow, one of her friends noted that he was immature rather than cold. He would never admit to having made mistakes. Even in 1970, in his introduction to *The Wartime Journals of Charles A. Lindbergh*, he "revealed a stubborn adherence to the beliefs he had voiced decades earlier," and refused to recant (Berg, 1998, p. 545).

Motor Skills

Lindbergh showed poor penmanship as a boy but otherwise displayed motor skills of a very high order throughout his life; therefore, he did not meet this particular criterion of Asperger Syndrome. He could shoot accurately at the age of 7, and learned to drive a car at the age of 11. At the university he performed dangerous motorbike stunts and, of course, his prowess as an aviator is unquestioned: "sharp-sighted and coordinated, with quick reflexes, Lindbergh proved to be a natural pilot" (Berg, 1998, p. 65).

Conclusion

We believe there is strong evidence to suggest that Charles Lindbergh had Asperger Syndrome, especially in terms of his social behavior, obsessiveness, lack of empathy, and need for control.

CHAPTER 20

Kurt Gödel
(1906–1978)

The mathematician and logician Kurt Friedrich Gödel was born on April 28, 1906, in Brünn, Austria-Hungary (now Brno, Czech Republic). He went to school in Brünn and studied mathematics at the

University of Vienna, going on to teach there from 1933 to 1938. In 1940, he immigrated to the United States, where he became a member of the Institute for Advanced Study at Princeton University, and later professor of mathematics. He married Adele Porkert in 1938, and became a U.S. citizen in 1948. Having almost died of a bleeding ulcer in 1951, he survived until January 14, 1978, when he died of self-starvation due to fear of poisoning. Like Ludwig Wittgenstein, his work was mainly published posthumously.

Dawson (1997) described Gödel as a "reclusive genius whose work has generally been considered abstruse and whose life, combining elements of rationality and psychopathology, has been the subject more of rumor than of concrete factual knowledge." Dawson continued, "There is, however, no doubt that Gödel's discoveries have been of the utmost importance within mathematics, and there is a growing awareness of the impact they have had on our modern world view" (p. ix).

Gödel was "celebrated for his incompleteness theorems, the implications of which are far-reaching for the foundations of mathematics and computer science. The story of his life and work is that of a persistent quest for rationality in all things" (Dawson, 1999, p. 68). While the incompleteness theorems were of major importance, they were often misunderstood initially, however. According to Dawson (1999), Gödel was "a Platonist: he believed that in addition to objects, there exists a world of concepts to which humans have access by intuition. Thus, for him a statement would have a definite 'truth value' – be it true or not – whether or not it had been proved or was amenable to being empirically confirmed or refuted" (p. 68).

Family and Childhood

Kurt Gödel was the younger of the two children of Rudolf Gödel and Marianne Gödel (née Handschuh), who had married in 1901. His elder brother was also called Rudolf. Their father was a partner in a firm of weavers. According to the younger Rudolf, his parents' marriage was not a love match, although it was built on affection and sympathy. Marianne was far more cultured and better educated than her husband, who had a more serious and ponderous disposition (Dawson, 1997). Kurt Gödel's paternal grandfather, Josef, allegedly committed suicide.

Kurt was "an exceptionally inquisitive child. By the time he was four years old his parents and older brother had begun to call him 'der Herr Warum' (Mr. Why), and in an early family portrait he stares at the camera with an earnestly questioning gaze" (Dawson, 1997, p. 1); Dawson noted, "The picture that emerges (from various sources) is that of an earnestly serious, bright, and inquisitive child who was sensitive, often withdrawn or preoccupied, and who, already at an early age, exhibited certain signs of emotional instability" (p. 6) According to his brother, Kurt suffered a mild anxiety neurosis at about the age of 5. He also developed rheumatic fever as a child. Dawson described him as introverted, sensitive and somewhat sickly.

He was an excellent chess player. There was "a pattern of frequent excused absences" in his school reports, and in 1917 to 1918 he was exempted from physical education: He turned away from swimming and calisthenics, activities he had previously enjoyed, preferring to stay home and read" (Dawson, 1997, p. 14). A friend stated that his interest in mathematics and physics had already manifested itself at the age of 10.

Possible Indicators of Asperger Syndrome

Social Behavior

Gödel was a shy introvert. Even though he was involved with the Vienna Circle (a philosophical discussion group founded in the early 1920s by Moritz Schlick), which brought him in touch with philosophers of science and mathematicians, he rarely spoke at the Circle. Dawson (1997) described him as reticent, shy, and reclusive, and noted that he had few friends.

At the Vienna Circle, Gödel disagreed with its views, but "shied away from controversy … and so held back from open criticism of the Circle's tenets. As was his habit in such formal gatherings, he was content most of the time to listen to what others had to say, only occasionally interjecting incisive comments" (Dawson, 1997, p. 26).

Dawson (1997) pointed out,

> To persist in asking "unanswerable" questions can quickly lead to social isolation, for the questioner is more likely to be reckoned a crank than a genius. Indeed, to seek rationality in all things is, from a modern point of view, a profoundly *irrational* act. It is not just that causal determinism is in opposition to the contemporary scientific *Zeitgeist*. It is that there are seemingly insuperable obstacles to the rational explanation of much human behavior. Consequently,

an archrationalist who is determined, as Gödel was, to find hidden causes to account for such behavior is likely to become distrustful of human motives. (p. 2)

This is precisely what persons with Asperger Syndrome tend to do. Karl Menger (1981) described Gödel at the Vienna Circle as follows: "I never heard him take the floor ... He indicated interest solely by slight motions of the head – in agreement, skeptically or in disagreement ... His expression (oral as well as written) was always of the greatest precision and at the same time of exceeding brevity. In nonmathematical conversation he was very withdrawn" (pp. 1–2).

Again, all this is very typical of a person with Asperger Syndrome. Olga Taussky-Todd (1987) stated that Gödel

was well trained in all branches of mathematics and you could talk to him about any problem and receive an excellent response. If you had a particular problem in mind he would start by writing it down in symbols. He spoke slowly and very calmly and his mind was very clear ... It became slowly obvious ... that he was incredibly talented. His help was much in demand ... [and] he offered [it] whenever it was needed ... But he was very silent. (p. 31)

Narrow Interests/Obsessiveness

His brother attested that Gödel had, through independent study, already "mastered University Mathematics by his final Gymnasium [academic high school] years," much "to the astonishment of his teachers and fellow pupils" (Dawson, 1997, p. 24).

Gödel clearly was interested in mathematics and logic to the point of obsessiveness. Like Newton, he was often so obsessed by his work that he would forget to eat. Nonetheless, he did have other interests, including parapsychology, superstition, and sorcery. His range of intellectual concerns was exceptionally wide. He believed in telepathy and that there was a "high probability" that "elementary psychic factors" (as opposed to physical factors) might exist (Dawson, 1997, p. 30). He had a strong interest in comparative religion, and many books in his library were devoted to strange religious sects. This interest is not uncommon in persons with high-functioning autism. Having been reared a free-thinker, Gödel eventually became a religious believer. In 1975, he described his belief as theistic rather than pantheistic, following Leibniz rather than Spinoza (Dawson, 1997).

"Gödel's interest in foreign languages – at least their formal aspects – continued beyond his school years. His *Nachlaß* contains notebooks on Italian, Dutch, and Greek in addition to (Latin, French and English)" (Dawson, 1997, p. 15). At the age of 14 he read about Goethe's color theory and his conflict with Newton's ideas. In hindsight, Gödel thought that this had led indirectly to his choice of profession. The first author of this volume has known some patients with high-functioning autism to be absolutely fascinated by color, as were Newton and Wittgenstein.

Routines/Control

Gödel "retained almost every scrap of paper that crossed his desk, including library request slips, luggage tags, crank correspondence, and letters from autograph seekers and mathematical amateurs" (Dawson, 1997, p. 1).

According to Dawson (1997), "Throughout his life, he refused to accept the notion of fortuitous events. A few years before his death he declared, 'Every chaos is a wrong appearance,' and in an undated memorandum found among his papers after his death he listed fourteen principles he considered fundamental. First among them was ... 'The world is rational'" (p. 2).

Further, Dawson (1997) noted that one who is convinced of the underlying orderliness of the world is likely to be attracted to mathematics. As Gödel himself once wrote, "In the world of mathematics everything is well poised and in perfect order." But Gödel went further, asking, "Shouldn't the same be assumed (expected) for the world of reality, contrary to appearances?" (p. 2). This is what the person with Asperger Syndrome is trying to achieve.

Language/Humor

As we have seen, Gödel spoke several languages and does not appear to have had a problem with language in general. He does not appear to have shown much of a sense of humor.

Lack of Empathy

Gödel could show extreme lack of empathy. While not anti-Semitic, at times he displayed purblindness to the plight of European Jews in the Nazi era. When he met Gustav Bergmann, a Jew who had come to the United States to escape the Nazis, he asked "And what brings you to America, Herr Bergmann?" (Dawson, 1997, p. 97). Menger (1981) noted that although Gödel was well informed on politics in the 1930s, he lacked strong emotional engagement.

In 1939, Gödel returned to Vienna and was summoned for medical examination by the Nazi armed forces. He appears to have got himself into that position because he remained "oddly unmoved" by politics rather than through Nazi sympathies: Dawson (1999) points out that, "His lack of emotional engagement with people may have kept him from appreciating the significance of what was happening. He seemed oblivious to the fates befalling his colleagues and professors, many of whom were Jewish, and stayed immersed in his work while the world around him fell apart" (p. 72).

Wittgenstein was taking a fairly similar position at this time, including not reading newspapers. Gödel's behavior is also reminiscent of the way that the artist L. S. Lowry seemed barely aware of World War I (Fitzgerald, 2005).

Naivety/Childishness

Gödel was very naïve and often alienated people. His attitude was often legalistic.

According to Dawson (1997), "Gödel's choice of profession, his Platonism, his mental troubles, and much else about him may … be ascribed to a sort of arrested development. He was a genius, but he was also, in many respects, a man/child" (p. 2). Dean Montgomery, one of Gödel's colleagues, noted that "like a child, Gödel always needed to be looked after." Dawson (1997) goes on:

> Despite his prodigious intellect, he often exhibited a childlike naïveté. His tastes remained unsophisticated, and his well-being depended on the efforts of those who were willing to shield him from the out-

side world, to tolerate his sometimes bizarre behavior, and to see that he received treatment in times of physical and mental disability. (pp. 2–3)

Gödel behaved in a classically autistic fashion when he was being inducted as a U.S. citizen. According to Dawson, "the judge who swore him in made the unfortunate error of asking his opinion of the U.S. constitution and unleashed a pent-up lecture on its inconsistencies" (Dawson, 1999, p. 73). Few people apart from those with an autism spectrum disorder would have behaved in this way; that is, a "neurotypical" person would have realized that such behavior was inappropriate and potentially counterproductive under the circumstances.

Motor Skills

There does not appear to be evidence that Gödel had problems in this area.

Nonverbal Communication

We have little information on this, apart from the "earnestly questioning gaze" mentioned above, the "slight motions of the head" through which he expressed himself at the Vienna Circle, and the fact that he was myopic throughout his adult life.

Comorbidity

Gödel had a number of "mental breakdowns." According to Dawson (1999),

His problems seem to have started with hypochondria: he was obsessive about his diet and bowel habits and kept a daily record for two decades or more of his body temperature and milk of magnesia consumption. He had a fear of accidental and, in later years, deliberate poisoning. This phobia led him to avoid eating food, so that he became malnourished. At the same time, though, he ingested a variety of pills for an imaginary heart problem. (p. 71)

Another person with an autism spectrum disorder who had dietary problems that led to death was Simone Weil (Fitzgerald, 2005). Gödel's fear of poisoning related especially to "gases that might be escaping from his refrigerator" (Dawson, 1999, p. 111). There appears to have been a paranoid element to his personality. It is interesting that Newton went through a short paranoid period in 1693. Similarly, Newton also was a hypochondriac and sometimes had problems eating properly (White, 1997).

Gödel survived because Adele took an interest in him and looked after him, serving as his food taster, until she had a stroke towards the end of his life and died on February 4, 1981. "She shielded Gödel from the worst of his irrational fears and was often the only one who could persuade him to eat. More than anyone else, she was responsible for keeping him alive and productive" (Dawson, 1999, p. 71). If the Indian mathematician Srinivasa Ramanujan (Fitzgerald, 2004) had had a similar person with him when he went to Cambridge, it is quite likely that he would have lived longer.

Later in his life Gödel ignored a bleeding ulcer because of his mistrust of doctors and almost died. This was not unlike Andy Warhol's fear of death and of hospitals, which caused him to delay a routine operation to remove gallstones to the point where the condition became life-threatening (Warhol is thought to have had Asperger Syndrome; Fitzgerald, 2005). He became more and more withdrawn and emaciated as he got older.

Conclusion

It appears that Gödel meets the criteria for Asperger's disorder, which does not require abnormalities in language or motor problems.

CHAPTER 21

Paul Erdös
(1913–1996)

Paul Erdös (pronounced "air-dish"), who probably produced a greater number of scholarly mathematics papers than any other mathematician, had a major impairment in social relationships but showed extreme savant ability in mathematics. He appears to have met the criteria for Asperger Syndrome, as defined by Christopher Gillberg (1991), and for Asperger's disorder according to the American Psychiatric Association (1994) classification.

Life History

Paul Erdös was born in Budapest on March 26, 1913, the son of two high school mathematics teachers. Two of Erdös's siblings died of scarlet fever during his mother's prenatal hospitalization and delivery of him. His father fought in World War I; he was captured when Paul was 1-1/2 years old and spent six years in Siberia as a prisoner of war.

According to Hoffman (1998), Erdös first did mathematics at the age of 3. As his mother taught during the day, Erdös was raised by a German governess. He became proficient with numbers as a toddler by studying the calendar and figuring out how many days it would be before his mother was home for the holidays. At 4 he entertained himself by "computing crazy things like how long it would take a train to reach the Sun ... He amused his mother's friends by asking them how old they were and then calculating in his head how many seconds they had lived" (Hoffman, 1998, p. 66). There is no doubt that he was a mathematical prodigy. At 3 he could multiply three-digit numbers in his head, and at 4 he discovered negative numbers. "I told my mother," he recalled, "that if you take 250 from 100 you get −150" (Hoffman, 1998, p. 11).

For most of Erdös's childhood his mother kept him out of school, fearing that it was a source of deadly childhood contagions. He studied at home with a tutor, entered the University of Pazmany Peter in Budapest at the age of 17, and received his Ph.D. in mathematics four years later.

Erdös took drugs – Ritalin or Dexedrine – on a daily basis. On one occasion he gave them up for a month and could not do any work. They were probably treating his hyperkinetic disorder. For the last 25 years of his life, after the death of his mother, he worked 19-hour days, keeping himself fortified with 10 to 20 mg of Benzedrine or Ritalin.

He had no time for "frivolities" like sex, art, fiction, or movies; he had no wife or children, no job, no hobbies, not even a home: He lived out of a shabby suitcase and a drab orange plastic bag (Hoffman, 1998). He died on September 20, 1996, at the age of 83, having written or coauthored 1,475 academic papers.

Possible Indicators of Asperger Syndrome

Social Behavior

When he was 17 years old, Erdös was invited to meet another very young mathematician – Andrew Vázsonyi, age 14. According to Hoffman (1998), he arrived at the store where he was to meet Vázsonyi and knocked – and then he "dispensed with all introductions and conversational pleasantries and charged to the back." He said to Vázsonyi, "Give me a four-digit number." "2,532," Vázsonyi replied, and so the conversation went (p. 60). It is hardly surprising that the sales assistant in the store regarded him as a "weirdo." This lack of introduction was very similar to the manner of Ludwig Wittgenstein.

Erdös referred to non-mathematicians as trivial beings. Louise Straus, wife of the mathematician Ernst Straus, described how, when Erdös visited, he casually called other mathematicians from the area to come to their house too without asking permission. He would often go "outside to the pay phone and drop coins in it all night, calling mathematicians around the world" (Hoffman, 1998, p. 125).

Another friend whom Erdös used to visit, Tom Trotter, stated that Erdös would be wandering around the house at 4 a.m. and would come into his bedroom to ask whether his brain was open. This shows his serious social interactional difficulties and lack of empathy for others. People tolerated him because he was a fascinating genius and was extraordinarily stimulating to have around for a while – they never knew how long he would stay. He moved on when he had exhausted his host. His modus operandi was to show up on the doorstep of a fellow mathematician, declare that his brain was open, work with his host for a day or two, until he was bored or his host was run down, and then move on to another home ("another roof, another proof"). He had so few clothes that his hosts found themselves washing his socks and underwear several times a week (Hoffman, 1998).

Like many people with Asperger Syndrome, Erdös tended to get on with people younger than him, and indeed he helped many child mathematical prodigies.

In his 70s, Erdös told Vázsonyi that he had never had sex: "the privilege of pleasure in dealing with women has not been given to me." When he was 70, he told a journalist, "Basically, I have a psychological abnormality. I cannot stand sexual pleasure" (Hoffman, 1998, p. 139).

When his mother died, he grieved for her for many years. Persons with Asperger Syndrome often need a helper to smooth their path in life. Paul Erdös found this in Ron Graham, a mathematician who looked after much of his affairs and correspondence. He managed his finances and sent out copies of his papers when requested. Without this sort of unconditional help, Erdös would have been much less successful, particularly after his mother died, and would probably have got into trouble with state and other agencies due to naivety and lack of knowledge about how to manage the basic social environment, tax returns, and so on. Outside the world of mathematics, he was nearly helpless.

Erdös disliked touching, handshaking, and kissing. He obsessively washed his hands 50 times a day for fear of germs. Nevertheless, he had a naïve trust in others. He was enormously generous to people in need and to poor people, always giving them money. On one occasion, when he won the Wolf Prize, he kept only $720 of the $50,000 for himself.

He had no problem in communicating with people on an intellectual (i.e., mathematical) level, and had a total of 485 coauthors over the years. At mathematical conferences, he would work on problems in a hotel room with four or five other mathematicians rather than going to the formal sessions. He was always on the lookout for people who had a spark of genius whom he could work with. He was given the opportunity to work on the atomic bomb during World War II but refused to sign a paper saying that he would not talk about the bomb after the war, showing a lack of empathy and respect for authority. This was a great loss for the Los Alamos project and also denied Erdös an opportunity to work with many of the best mathematicians in the world.

Narrow Interests/Obsessiveness

Referring to Paul Erdös, the mathematician Joel Spencer stated, "Mathematical truth is immutable; it lies outside physical reality ... This is our belief; this is our core motivating force. Yet our attempts to describe this belief to our nonmathematical friends are akin to describing the Almighty to an atheist. Paul embodied this belief in mathematical truth. His enormous talents and energies were given entirely to the Temple of Mathematics. He harbored no doubts about the importance ... of his quest" (Hoffman, 1998, p. i). The *Economist* wrote, "To find another life this century as intensely devoted to abstraction one must reach back to Ludwig Wittgenstein ... who stripped his life bare for philosophy. But whereas Wittgenstein discarded his family fortune as a form of self-torture, Mr. Erdös gave away much of the money he earned because he simply did not need it ... And where Wittgenstein was driven by near suicidal compulsions, Mr. Erdös simply constructed his life to extract the maximum amount of happiness" (Hoffman, 1998, p. i). His only interest in life was mathematics, and he lived out of a suitcase for much of his life. Very aptly, the title of Hoffman's biography of Erdös is *The Man Who Loved Only Numbers.*

Erdös thought that private property was a nuisance and would interfere with his mathematical focus. He felt the same way about personal relationships of a non-mathematical kind, and a family. He always carried notebooks with him, like Ludwig Wittgenstein and Ramanujan, to jot down his mathematical thoughts. A colleague took him to the Johnson Space Center to see rockets but found that Erdös didn't even look up. Another mathematician dragged him to the Museum of Modern Art in New York: "We showed him Matisse, but he would have nothing to do with it. After a few minutes we ended up sitting in the Sculpture Gardens doing mathematics" (Hoffman, 1998, p. 23). G. B. Kolata wrote, "Not only has Erdös dispensed with most of the encumbrances of daily living but he has also dispensed with many of the pleasantries that could take him from his mathematics. For example, Erdös keeps his telephone conversations brief if not curt, unless he is talking about mathematics" (Hoffman, 1998, p. 21). Stanislaw Ulam of the University of Florida wrote that Erdös often walked into a room and immediately began discussing mathematics without explaining his presence or exchanging greetings first.

According to Hoffman (1998), "part of his mathematical success stemmed from his willingness to ask fundamental questions, to ponder critically things that others had taken for granted" (p. 21). Ludwig Wittgenstein was also able to see problems that others had missed. Hoffman also noted, "Erdös was a mathematical monk. He renounced physical pleasure and material possessions for an ascetic, contemplative life, a life devoted to a single narrow mission: uncovering mathematical truth" (p. 25). For Erdös, "Mathematics is the surest way to immortality. If you make a big discovery in mathematics, you will be remembered after everyone else will be forgotten" (p. 29). Clearly, there is a narcissistic aspect to this statement, and narcissism is a feature of Asperger Syndrome.

According to Hoffman (1998), "Mathematics, in its abstractness and observation of formal rules, has been likened to chess. Both activities demand of their practitioners deep concentration, the tuning out of one's surroundings to focus on the formal structure at hand" (p. 30). This definition of the process of mathematics has parallels with definitions of autism, in terms of narrow focus and de-emphasis of surroundings/context.

Hoffman (1998) quoted Erdös as follows: "In a way, mathematics is the only infinite human activity. It is conceivable that humanity could eventually learn everything in physics or biology. But humanity certainly won't ever be able to find out everything in mathematics, because the subject is infinite. Numbers themselves are infinite. That is why mathematics is really my only interest" (p. 60). It is interesting that Ramanujan, another mathematician of genius who probably had Asperger Syndrome (Fitzgerald, 2004), was also fascinated by infinity.

Routines/Control

Erdös imposed routines on himself and others. If people were not mathematicians, he did not relate to them. As mentioned, he had a routine of moving from one mathematician to the next, and working on mathematical problems with them. He completely controlled them, and they were willing to be controlled by him because he was such a fascinating character and so stimulating intellectually. Ludwig Wittgenstein had similar power of control over people. Erdös also had such control over himself that he could play a board game and conduct a mathematical proof at the same time.

Language/Humor

Erdös had an idiosyncratic and amusing vocabulary – to communicate with him one had to learn his language. For example, when he asked someone "When did you arrive?" he meant "When were you born?" Children were "epsilons" (the Greek letter epsilon being used in mathematics to stand for small quantities), God was the "SF" (Supreme Fascist); other terms he used were "bosses" (women), "slaves" (men), "captured" (married), "liberated" (divorced), "recaptured" (remarried), "noise" (music), "poison" (alcohol), "preaching" (lecturing), "Sam" or "Samland" (USA), "Joe" or "Joedom" (Soviet Union), "died" (stopped doing mathematics), "left" (died). "Wine, women and song" thus became "poison, bosses and noise." Melvyn Nathanson described him as "the Bob Hope of mathematics, a kind of vaudeville performer who told the same jokes and the same stories a thousand times" (Hoffman, 1998, p. 11).

Naivety/Childishness

A friend said that Erdös had "a childlike tendency to make his reality overtake yours" (Hoffman, 1998, p. 7). As we have seen, he was virtually helpless in the everyday world, relying on friends to drive him around, cook his meals, wash his clothes, and so on.

Motor Clumsiness

Erdös was very clumsy and walked in an awkward fashion – his gait was described as "apelike." He could never figure out how to shut off the faucets on a shower, or to deal with a sash window so that it wouldn't come crashing down. Even as an adult he had trouble tying his shoes; on one occasion he asked people at a party to do it for him. He was 21 years old when he buttered his first slice of bread.

Conclusion

Paul Erdös meets the criteria for Asperger Syndrome, as set out by Christopher Gillberg (1991), and also the criteria for Asperger's disorder, as set out by the American Psychiatric Association (1994). He shows the classic relationship difficulty of persons with Asperger Syndrome, with the savant special abilities that about 10 percent of persons with autism demonstrate. It is clear that the enhanced ability to focus can provide great dividends in relation to a creative activity such as mathematics.

Conclusion

We hope the reader has enjoyed our re-examination of the lives of 21 prominent creative individuals, as well as the overview of issues concerning creativity, genius, and autism offered in the Introduction. On the basis of the available biographical material, we have suggested diagnoses of Asperger Syndrome (or the less restrictively defined Asperger's disorder; American Psychiatric Association, 1994) in most cases. The level of our confidence in these diagnoses varies from person to person, as outlined in the conclusion to each chapter.

Thus, it seems likely that Archimedes had Asperger Syndrome, although the paucity of data renders a firm conclusion impossible. There is no doubt that many leading mathematicians have had Asperger Syndrome; however, our analysis suggests that hyperkinetic syndrome may be a better diagnosis for Charles Babbage, for example. While he displayed some typical Asperger traits, he seems to have lacked social impairment. Of the other subjects, an entire book has already been devoted to the thesis that one of them – Thomas Jefferson – had autism (Ledgin, 2000; we concur), while a biography of Henry Cavendish (Jungnickel & McCormmach, 1996) identifies autistic-like traits without explicitly identifying him as autistic. Others to whom we can ascribe Asperger Syndrome with reasonable confidence include Isaac Newton, Gregor Mendel, Gerard Manley Hopkins, H. G. Wells, Albert Einstein, Charles de Gaulle, Norbert Wiener, Charles Lindbergh, and Paul Erdös. Those to whom we assign the less circumscribed diagnosis of Asperger's disorder (which does not require abnormalities of speech and language nor motor clumsiness; APA, 1994) include Charles Darwin, Thomas "Stonewall" Jackson, Nikola Tesla, David Hilbert, John Broadus Watson, Bernard Law Montgomery, Alfred C. Kinsey, and Kurt Gödel. Darwin may also have shown schizoid personality in childhood. A lack of information on abnormalities of speech and language or motor clumsiness does not necessarily mean that such abnormalities were not present – these individuals may, in fact, have had Asperger Syndrome.

In many cases, one can easily discern a link between psychopatho-logical traits and great creativity. In the case of Isaac Newton, whom we describe as the greatest genius of the past thousand years, creative output was enhanced by social detachment and an obses-sive, driven approach to his work. A perpetual loner who imposes extreme control on himself and others may achieve greatness where a more balanced, sociable person with similar intellectual resources would not. Intense focus on a narrow interest can produce a great deal of new knowledge. An autism spectrum disorder, in some respects, can be seen as advantageous, even if the vast majority of persons with autism are not geniuses (similarly to the vast majority of "neurotypicals"). Certainly, particular autistic traits can be chan-neled in a positive way in non-geniuses – this is largely a matter of perspective, and of rejecting an entirely negative connotation of the word "autism." We hope that this book will help to foster a more positive view of persons with autism among the general community.

References

Adams, W. H. (1983). *Jefferson's Monticello*. New York: Abbeville Press.

American Psychiatric Association. (1994). *Diagnostic and statistical manual of mental disorders, 4th edition*. Washington, DC: Author.

Asperger, H. (1944). Die "autisticheen psychopathen" im kindersalter. *Archiv for Psychiatrie und Nervenkrankheiten, 117,* 76-136.

Atkinson, R. C. (1993). Introduction. *Ciba foundation symposium 178* (pp. 1-4). Chichester, UK: Wiley.

Bailey A. (1993). Editorial: The biology of autism. *Psychological Medicine, 23,* 7-11.

Bell, E. T. (1986). *Men of mathematics*. New York: Simon & Schuster.

Berenson, B. (1954). *The Italian painters of the Renaissance*. London: Phaidon.

Berg, A. S. (1998). *Lindbergh*. London: Macmillan.

Berry, A. J. (1960). *Henry Cavendish: His life and scientific work*. London: Hutchinson.

Bevin, A. (1996). *Lost victories: The military genius of Stonewall Jackson*. Secaucus, NJ: Blue and Gray Press.

Bickley, F. (1911). *The Cavendish family*. London: Constable.

Bragg, M. (1998). *On giants' shoulders*. London: Hodder & Stoughton.

Brett-James, A. (1984). *Conversations with Montgomery*. London: William Kimber.

Brewster, D. (1855). *Memoirs of the life, writings, and discoveries of Sir Isaac Newton, Vol. II.* Edinburgh: Thomas Constable.

Brougham, H. (1845). *Lives of men of letters and science who flourished in the time of George III.* Philadelphia: Carey & Hart.

Brown, L. (Ed.). (1993). *The New Shorter Oxford English Dictionary* (2 vols.). Oxford: Oxford University Press.

Brown, P. D., & Schweizer, K. W. (Eds). (1982). *The Devonshire diary: William Cavendish, 4th Duke of Devonshire, memoranda on state of affairs, 1759–1762.* Camden Fourth Series, Volume 27. London: Royal Historical Society.

Buckley, K. W. (1989). *Mechanical man: John Broadus Watson and the beginnings of behaviorism.* New York: Guilford Press.

Burstein, A. (1995). *The inner Jefferson: Portrait of a grieving optimist.* Charlottesville: University Press of Virginia.

Butler, S. (1917). *The notebooks of Samuel Butler.* New York: Dutton.

Buxton, H. W. (1988). *Memoir of the life and labours of the late Charles Babbage Esq. F.R.S.*, Vol. 13, The Charles Babbage Institute Reprint Series for the History of Computing. Cambridge, MA: Tomash.

Chandler, D. L. (1994). *The Jefferson conspiracies.* New York: William Morrow.

Cheney, M. (1981). *Tesla: Man out of time.* Englewood Cliffs, NJ: Prentice Hall.

Clark, Ronald W. (1971). *Einstein: The life and times.* New York: World Publishing Co.

Colagelo, N., & Kerr, B. (1992). The Iowa inventiveness inventory: Towards a measure of mechanical inventiveness. *Creativity Research Journal, 5,* 157–163.

Cox, C. M. (1926). *Genetics studies of genius, Volume II: The early mental traits of three hundred geniuses.* Stanford, CA: Stanford University Press.

Dawson, J. W., Jr. (1997). *Logical dilemmas: The life and work of Kurt Gödel.* Wellesley, MA: AK Peters.

Dawson, J. W., Jr. (1999, June). Gödel and the limits of logic. *Scientific American, 280*(6), 68–73.

References

Deglar, C. N. (1991). *In search of human nature*. Oxford: Oxford University Press.

Desmond, A., & Moore, J. (1992). *Darwin*. London: Penguin Books.

Devlin, K. (2000). *The maths gene: Why everyone has it, but most people don't use it*. London: Weidenfeld & Nicolson.

Douglas, H. K. (1940). *I rode with Stonewall*. London: Putnam.

Ellis, J. J. (1997). *American sphinx: The character of Thomas Jefferson*. New York: Alfred A. Knopf.

Feldman, D. H. (1986). *Nature's gambit: Child prodigies and the development of human potential*. New York: Basic Books.

Fitzgerald, M. (1999). Did Isaac Newton have Asperger's syndrome? *European Child and Adolescent Psychiatry, 8*, 204.

Fitzgerald, M. (2004). *Autism and creativity: Is there a link between autism in men and exceptional ability?* Hove, UK: Brunner-Routledge.

Fitzgerald, M. (2005). *The genesis of artistic creativity: Asperger's syndrome and the arts*. London: Jessica Kingsley.

Fölsing, A. (1997). *Albert Einstein: A biography* (E. Osers, Trans.). London: Viking.

Frith, U. (1989). *Autism: Explaining the enigma*. Oxford: Blackwell.

Frith, U. (Ed.). (1991). *Autism and Asperger's syndrome*. Cambridge: Cambridge University Press.

Gagné, F. (1998). A biased survey and interpretation of the nature–nurture literature. *Behavioral and Brain Sciences, 21*(3), 415.

Galton, F. (1896). *Hereditary genius: An inquiry into its laws and consequences*. London: Macmillan.

Gardner, H. (1980). *Artful scribbles: The significance of children's drawings*. New York: Basic Books.

Gardner, H. (1997). *Extraordinary minds: Portraits of exceptional individuals and an examination of our extraordinariness*. London: Weidenfeld & Nicholson.

Ghiselin, B. (1952). Introduction. In B. Ghiselin (Ed.), *The creative process: A symposium* (pp. 20–21). Berkeley: University of California Press.

Gillberg, C. (1991). Clinical and neurobiological aspects in six family studies of Asperger's syndrome. In U. Frith (Ed.), *Autism and Asperger's syndrome* (pp. 122–146). Cambridge: Cambridge University Press.

Gillberg, C. (1996). *Asperger's syndrome and high functioning autism.* Blake Marsh Lecture, Quarterly Meeting of the Royal College of Psychiatrists, Stratford-upon-Avon, UK.

Goldberger, P. (1999, February). Why Washington slept here. *The New Yorker, 74,* 88.

Grandin, T. (1986). *Emergence: Labeled autistic.* New York: Warner Books.

Gregory, R. (1987). *Oxford companion to the mind.* Oxford: Oxford University Press.

Hall, A. R. (1996). *Isaac Newton: Adventure in thought.* Cambridge: Cambridge University Press.

Hamilton, N. (1981). *Monty: The making of a general 1887–1942.* London: Hamish Hamilton.

Hart, M. (1993). *The 100.* London: Simon & Schuster.

Hart-Davis, R. (1952) *Hugh Walpole: A Biography.* New York: Macmillan.

Heller, K. A., & Ziegler, A. (1998). Experience is no improvement over talent. *Behavioral and Brain Sciences, 21*(3), 417.

Henig, R. M. (2001). *A monk and two peas.* London: Phoenix.

Henry, W. D. (1979). Stonewall Jackson – The soldier eccentric. *Practitioner, 223,* 580–587.

Hoffman, P. (1998). *The man who loved only numbers.* London: Fourth Estate.

Horne, A. (with Montgomery, D.). (1994). *The lonely leader.* London: Macmillan.

Howe, M. J. A. (1999). *Genius explained.* Cambridge: Cambridge University Press.

Iles, G. (1906). *Inventors at work.* New York: Doubleday.

Jenkins, R. (1993). *Portraits and miniatures*. London: Macmillan.

Johnson, D. (2000, July 21). *Times Literary Supplement,* pp. 3–4.

Jones, J. H. (1997). *Alfred C. Kinsey: A public/private life.* New York: W. W. Norton.

Jungnickel, C., & McCormmach, R. (1996). *Cavendish: The experimental life.* Philadelphia: The American Philosophical Society.

Keynes, J. M. (1947). Newton the man. Royal Society, *Newton Tercentenary Celebrations.* Cambridge: Cambridge University Press.

Lacouture, J. (1990). *De Gaulle: The rebel 1890-1944.* London: Collins Harvill.

Lacouture, J. (1991). *De Gaulle: The ruler 1945-1970.* London: Harvill.

Ledgin, N. (2000). *Diagnosing Jefferson.* Arlington, TX: Future Horizons.

Levinson, N. (1966). Wiener's life. *Bulletin of the American Mathematical Society, 72* (special issue), 1-32.

Lykken, D. T. (1998). The genetics of genius. In A. Steptoe (Ed.), *Genius and the mind: Studies of creativity and temperament* (pp. 15–37). Oxford: Oxford University Press.

Lykken, D. T., Gue, M., Tellegen, A., & Bouchard, T. (1992). Emergenesis: Genetic traits that may not run in families. *American Psychologist, 47*(12), 1072.

MacKenzie, N., & MacKenzie, J. (1973). *The life of H. G. Wells: The time traveller.* London: Weidenfeld & Nicolson.

MacKinnon, D. W. (1978). *In search of human effectiveness: Identifying and developing creativity.* Buffalo, NY: Creative Education Association.

Magnusson, M. (Ed.). (1990). *Chambers biographical dictionary,* 5th ed. Edinburgh: W & R Chambers.

Maslow, A. (1971). *The farther reaches of human nature.* New York: Viking.

Mauriac, F. (1966). *De Gaulle.* London: Bodley Head.

McLaughlin, J. (1988). *Jefferson and Monticello: The biography of a builder.* New York: Holt.

Mead, M. (1949). *Male and female*. New York: William Morrow.

Menger, K. (1981). *Recollections of Kurt Gödel*. Unpublished typescript, published in revised form as *Memories of Kurt Gödel*. In L. Golland, B. McGuinness & A. Sklar (Eds.), (1994). *Reminiscences of the Vienna circle and the mathematical colloquium* (pp. 200–236). Dordrecht, The Netherlands: Kluwer.

Montgomery, B. (1987). *A field marshal in the family*. London: Javelin Books.

Moorehead, A. (1946). *Montgomery*. London: Hamish Hamilton.

Murray, P. (Ed.). (1989). *Genius: The history of an idea*. Oxford: Basil Blackwell.

Perkins, D. N. (1981). *The mind's best work*. Cambridge, MA: Harvard University Press.

Peterson, M. D. (1970). *Thomas Jefferson and the new nation*. New York: Oxford University Press.

Peterson, M. D. (Ed.). (1984). *Thomas Jefferson: Writings*. New York: The Library of America.

Plomin, R. (1998). Genetic influence and cognitive abilities. *Behavioral and Brain Sciences, 21*(3), 420-421.

Polya, G. (1969, September). Some mathematicians I have known. *American Mathematical Monthly*, 747.

Radford, J. (1990). *Child prodigies and exceptional early achievers*. Hemel Hempstead, UK: Harvester Wheatsheaf.

Reid, C. (1970). *Hilbert*. London: George Allen Unwin.

Scar, S., & McCartney, K. (1983). How people make their own environments: A theory of genotype–environment effects. *Child Development, 54*, 424-435.

Shapin, S. (1991). A scholar and a gentleman: The problematic identity of the scientific practitioner in early modern England. *History of Science, 29*, 279-327.

Simonton, D. K. (1991). Emergence and realization of genius: The lives and works of 120 classical composers. *Journal of Personality and Social Psychology, 61*, 829-840.

Simonton, D. K. (1994). *Greatness: Who makes history and why*. New York: Guilford Press.

References

Simonton, D. K. (1998). Defining and finding talent: Data and a multiplicative model? *Behavioral and Brain Sciences, 21*(3), 424.

Ssucharewa, G. E. (1926). Die schizoiden Psychopathien im Kindes-alter. *Monatschrift für Psychiatrie und Neurologie, 60,* 235-261.

Storr, A. (1988). *Solitude.* New York: The Free Press.

Storr, A. (1989). Genius and psychoanalysis: Freud, Jung and the concept of personality. In P. Murray (Ed.), *Genius: The history of an idea* (pp. 213–232). Oxford: Basil Blackwell.

Strathern, P. (1998). *Archimedes and the fulcrum.* London: Arrow Books.

Swade, D. (2000). *The cogwheel brain: Charles Babbage and the quest to build the first computer.* London: Little, Brown.

Swezey, K. M. (1927, October). Nikola Tesla. *Psychology,* p. 60.

Taussky-Todd, O. (1987). Remembrances of Kurt Gödel. In P. Weingartner & L. Schmetterer (Eds.), *Gödel remembered* (pp. 31–41). Naples, Italy: Bibliopolis.

Taylor, A. J. P. (1965). *English history 1914-1945.* London: Dent.

Terman, L. M. (1917). The intelligence quotient of Francis Galton in childhood. *American Journal of Psychology, 28,* 209-215.

Tesla, N. (1919). My inventions. *Electrical Experimenter* (May, June, July, October, republished by Skolska Kanjiiga, Zagreb, Yugoslavia, 1977, p. 30)

Turnbull, H. (Ed.). (1959). *Correspondence of Isaac Newton,* Vol. 1. Cambridge: Cambridge University Press.

Ulam, S. (1983). *Adventures of a mathematician.* New York: Scribner's Sons.

Wang, H. (1987). *Reflections on Kurt Gödel.* Cambridge, MA: MIT Press.

Watson, J. B. (1924). *Behaviourism.* Chicago: University of Chicago Press.

Watt, J. (1846). *Correspondence of the late James Watt on his discovery of the theory of the composition of water.* London: John Murray.

Wells, H. G. (1934). *Experiment in autobiography: Discoveries and conclusions of a very ordinary brain (since 1866).* London: Victor Gollancz.

White, M., & Gribbin, J. (1995). *Darwin: A life in science.* London: Simon & Schuster.

White, M. (1997). *Isaac Newton: The last sorcerer.* London: Fourth Estate.

White, N. (1992). *Hopkins: A literary biography.* Oxford: Clarendon Press.

White, N. (2002). *Hopkins in Ireland.* Dublin: University College Dublin Press.

Whitehead, A. N. (1948). *The nature of mathematics.* London: Oxford University Press.

Wiener, N. (1956). *I am a mathematician: The later life of a prodigy.* New York: Doubleday.

Wilson, G. (1851). *The life of the honourable Henry Cavendish.* London: Cavendish Society.

Wing, L. (1981). HFA/ASP: A clinical account. *Psychological Medicine, 11,* 115-129.

Wolff, S. (1995). *Loners: The life path of unusual children.* London: Routledge.

Wolff, S. (1998). Schizoid personality in childhood: The links with schizophrenia spectrum disorders. In E. Schopler, G. Mesibov & L. Kunce (Eds.), *Asperger's syndrome or high-functioning autism?* (pp. 123–145). New York: Plenum.

Notes

1. Simone Weil is a documented example of a prominent woman with Asperger Syndrome; see Fitzgerald, M. (2005). *The Genesis of Artistic Creativity: Asperger's Syndrome and the Arts*. London: Jessica Kingsley.

2. According to White (1997, pp. 1–2), of Newton's earlier biographers, William Stukeley (who wrote *Memoirs of Sir Isaac Newton's Life* in the 1720s) was 'blinkered by adoration … and saw Newton as a demigod, almost immortal and utterly without fault'; Sir David Brewster's *Memoirs of the Life, Writings, and Discoveries of Sir Isaac Newton*, published in 1855, continued in the same vein, being "tarnished by the author's lack of objectivity."

3. Arianism was a "heretical" doctrine asserting that Christ was not of one substance with God.

4. White (1997, p. 127) also notes that Carl Jung brought this idea into the twentieth century. Jung "was fascinated with the psychology of alchemy and came to the conclusion that alchemical emblems bore a close relationship to dream imagery – an observation which eventually led him to the concept of the collective unconscious."

5. Edward Thorpe to Joseph Larmor, 7 Feb. 1920, Larmor Papers, Royal Society Library, 1972.

6. Young, T. Life of Cavendish, in H. Cavendish, *Scientific Papers, 1*, 444.

7. Horace Walpole to Horace Mann, 4 June 1749. W. S. Lewis et al. (Eds.), In *Horace Walpole's Correspondence* (1937–83, vol. 15, p. 317). New Haven, CT: Yale University Press.

8. This was the title of the first published biography of Babbage, by M. Mosely (1964).

9. In his book *Anticipations of the Reaction of Mechanical and Scientific Progress upon Human Life and Thought*. He later claimed to have invented the military tank, and complained bitterly when he was not consulted on the design of tanks during World War I, even considering legal action.

10. For reasons outlined in the Preface, when we examine links between creativity, genius, and forms of autism, we soon find that we are dealing almost exclusively with men rather than women.

Index

P.O. Box 23173
Shawnee Mission, Kansas 66283-0173
www.asperger.net